# PROPHET WITHOUT PORTFOLIO

# PROPHET WITHOUT PORTFOLIO

*A Study and Interpretation of the Prophecy
of Second Isaiah*

By

## VIRGIL H. TODD

*Professor of Old Testament
Memphis Theological Seminary*

THE CHRISTOPHER PUBLISHING HOUSE
NORTH QUINCY, MASSACHUSETTS

PRINTED IN

THE UNITED STATES OF AMERICA

*To*
*Irene and Don*

# PREFACE

The unknown prophet of the Exile has too long been overshadowed by the eighth-century prophet (Isaiah of Jerusalem), to whose work the Second Isaiah's book is attached. Thus, the day has arrived for this prophet of the Exile to come into his own; for his work to be re-evaluated and to gain the recognition and level of appreciation which it rightly deserves.

Although we do not have any material or first-hand knowledge about the background or personal history of this one whose work we label "Second Isaiah," a man without even a name of his own, without credentials, or (as the title of this work suggests) *a prophet without portfolio,* a study of his book supplies us those data which are the most significant. These data reflect the quality of his life and thought and, at the same time, give evidence of his gifted literary ability and theological understanding. The prophet's work, in a real sense, represents a maturing of prophetic thought in Israel. The finesse and quality of the poetry set it apart as some of the best in the Old Testament, and the religious concepts rank equally as high.

This prophet, however, has too often been maligned by those who have failed to interpret his poetry and symbolism correctly. To many so-called interpreters, he

9

has been little more than a "morally deficient sky-gazer," a prophet who took flight in phantasy. Because of this gross misunderstanding, the present writer has felt the need for another treatment of this important book, which (hopefully) will offer an interpretation that will enable this prophet to achieve a new luster and stature in the eyes of the student, minister, teacher or Christian layman who can recognize his tremendous contribution to the Judeo-Christian religion.

It is the present writer's view that the prophecy of Second Isaiah must be interpreted eschatologically. When this is done, the prophecy that has hitherto remained inexplicable for many students of the Bible takes on a new dimension of meaning. In fact, it is the present writer's belief that the basic outline of Old Testament theology is reflected in the work of this prophet of the Exile. In other words, the themes which are commonly considered in a theology of the Old Testament are, for the most part, delineated in Isaiah 40-55. Some of the principal ones are, consequently, singled out and discussed in the body of this work.

It has been the author's intention to prepare a serious study of this unnamed prophet's work, a study that would not embarrass the scholar and, at the same time, would not be unduly difficult for the layman or church school teacher who desires to enter upon an ambitious learning experience. Consequently, copious references and footnotes have been added for the benefit of the reader who desires to pursue further the subject at hand.

The present writer's indebtedness to Old Testament scholarship is evidenced by the frequent references made to the works of others. But to no one scholar is he more indebted than to his former teacher, Dr. J. Philip Hyatt, professor of Old Testament, Vanderbilt Divinity School, who helped to open to this writer many vistas of understanding and to enhance his interest and appreciation for the Old Testament as a depository of faith and experience for the covenant people.

Unless otherwise specified, scripture passages throughout this work are quoted from the Revised Standard Version.

*Virgil H. Todd*

Memphis, Tennessee
January, 1972

# CONTENTS

*Chapter 1*

## THE SCOPE OF THE PROPHECY

### I. Introduction

The initial task in a work such as this is to define sharply the Biblical materials which are to be considered in the subsequent treatment. This, ordinarily, would pose a very small problem, but with the prophet whose work is to engage our attention the situation is different. In fact, throughout the history of Biblical criticism (and even unto the present time), as we shall see below, scholars have failed to agree upon what constitutes the work of Second Isaiah. Thus, it remains for us to determine pointedly what portion of the Book of Isaiah can be attributed to this unnamed and unknown prophet of the Exile.

Before isolating these specific passages, however, it will be helpful to review the way in which the whole prophecy of Isaiah has been handled by Biblical scholars.

### II. History of Criticism

The unity of the Book of Isaiah has long been questioned. As early as the middle of the twelfth century Ibn Ezra had expressed some doubts about Isaiah's being the author of chapters 40-66.[1] More serious doubts developed in the eighteenth century. In 1775, J.C. Doederlein published his commentary on *Esaias,* in which he recognized two distinct works. His hypothesis was that chapters 40-66 originated with a later poet. This hypothesis was later accepted by J.G. Eichhorn who, between 1780-1783, helped to popularize this position, a view that is widely held today, although with various shades of difference.[2]

The foregoing view (Eichhorn's) was generally accepted among the critical scholars for a little over one hundred years. During this time chapters 40-66 were designated by the name Deutero-Isaiah. But in 1892, Bernhard Duhm, a German scholar, wrote a brilliant commentary on the Book of Isaiah in which he set forth a new theory.[3] He contended that chapters 40-66 were not from the pen of just one anonymous poet, but from three different authors. The oldest, Duhm says, is the so-called Deutero-Isaiah, the author of chapters 40-55, with the exception of the later insertions. He wrote around 540 B.C., probably in Phoenicia. Later, after the Exile, the Servant passages were added. They have some similarity, Duhm contends, with the Book of Jeremiah and the Book of Job. Their relationship with Deutero-Isaiah, however, is not known. But still, Duhm holds, Second Isaiah must have taken consideration of them. Finally, Duhm alleges that chapters 56-66 were written shortly before the time of Nehemiah, probably in Jerusalem. This section he labels as Trito-Isaiah.[4]

Many present-day writers now accept Duhm's views, with of course certain modifications. In other words, a number of critics deny the homogeneity of Isaiah 40-66, and see two or more contributors to this work. It is

true that Duhm recognized the similarities between Deutero-Isaiah (chs. 40-55), and the last section (chs. 56-
66) which he labeled Trito-Isaiah. But he attributed this
similarity to the fact that chapters 56-66 were written
by disciples of Deutero-Isaiah, just as later critics have
held.[5]

Otto Eissfeldt also recognizes a strong relationship
between chapters 40-55 and 56-66, but he says that it
is not less than that between chapters 1-39 and chapters
40-55.

Even though there are recognized "stylistic and the-
matic resemblances," Eissfeldt concludes that only chapters 1-39 are from the Isaiah of the eighth century.[6]

If one accepts this conclusion, he may nevertheless
wonder why both of these sections are included in the
Book of Isaiah. Eissfeldt offers two likely conjectures:
(1) mechanical accident; (2) the strong affinity between
chapters 1-35 (39) and 40-66. Again, as he says, it is
possible that chapters 40-55 and 56-66 stood in the same
roll after Isaiah 1-39 as anonymous prophecies, and gradually these anonymous parts were attributed to Isaiah.[7]

T. K. Cheyne, in dealing with the same question, conjectures that the later, post-exilic editor may have felt
that the genuine work of Isaiah of Jerusalem "was but a
meagre monument of so great a prophet." At the same
time, he may have feared that without the status of a
"name," the great prophecy of restoration would fade
into oblivion. Hence, without actually asserting that
chapters 40-66 were from the pen of Isaiah, the editor
was not unwilling for the future readers of the book to
take such for granted.[8]

With reference to Isaiah 40-66, it should be noted that there are similarities between chapters 40-55 and 56-66. But the dissimilarities are just as marked. The most obvious difference between these two divisions is that in some passages in this latter section the Temple is evidently standing (56:5ff.; 60:7, 13), although the walls of Jerusalem remain unbuilt (60:10). By inference, then, the date suggested is some time between 516 B.C. (the rebuilding of the Temple), and 444 B.C. (the coming of Nehemiah).[9]

James Muilenburg also adduces various arguments against the integrity of Isaiah 40-66. He, too, feels that the weightiest argument against the unity of this material is in the historical situation. Isaiah 40-55 presupposes that the Jewish community is in exile in Babylonia, whereas in chapters 56-66 Jerusalem is the obvious locus.

Furthermore, Isaiah 56-66 is preoccupied with Sabbath observance and fasting, things that are foreign to Isaiah 40-55. Finally, the eschatology of chapters 56-66 is more like chapters 34-35 than chapters 40-55.[10]

Even though there are many modern critics who discredit the integrity of Isaiah 40-66, there are still others who accept it and argue just as fervently in the support of their theories. The most outspoken champion of the unity of Isaiah 40-66 has been the eminent C. C. Torrey,[11] who maintains vigorously that Isaiah 40-55 and Isaiah 56-66 "are pieces out of the very same homogenious block."[12]

Torrey's theory rests upon a very dubious and ingenious system of interpretation (or so it appears to the present writer) which allows him rather arbitrarily to excise certain passages as "interpolations" when they fail to fit into this preconceived pattern of exegesis. Thus, in order to make the prophecy fit into the historical picture c. 400 B.C., Torrey contends that the mention of Cyrus (45:1; 44:28) represents interpolations. The same holds true, he says, for the names "Babylon" and "Chaldea" (43:14; 48:14; 48:20). Instead of the prophecies being addressed to the people in exile, Torrey holds that the prophecies in Second Isaiah have to do with the Jews in Palestine at a later period. The term "exile," he declares, is merely a figure used to describe the Jewish dispersion.

Accordingly, Isaiah 40-66, as well as Isaiah 34-35, constitute a unified whole of some twenty-seven poems, all written by a sublime poet, a "single commanding genius speaking throughout the whole."[13]

S. R. Driver is rather emphatic in his view relative to Second Isaiah. He says that chapters 40-66 "form a continuous prophecy, dealing throughout with a common theme, viz. *Israel's restoration from exile in Babylon.*"[14]

Louis Finkelstein emphasizes Deutero-Isaiah's versatility. He says further that "from such a genius one would naturally expect differences of approach and expression which might suggest difference of authorship."[15]

The above discussion reveals that modern critical scholarship does not accept the total unity of the Book of Isaiah, even though some writers hold to the integrity of Isaiah 40-66. This, however, does not constitute the entire picture of scholarship. A number of conservative scholars hold to the unquestioned unity of the *whole* Book of Isaiah (chapters 1-66), and vigorously deny that the prophecy represents a compilation of compilations or (what is commonly called) a prophetic anthology. Merrill F. Unger's work may well be representative of this conservative school.

Unger takes into consideration the criteria which we shall mention in our next section and refutes each one. In addition to finding weaknesses in what he calls "the critics' arguments," he lists several other reasons for holding to the unity of the book. They are as follows: (1) "The New Testament witnesses to the Isaianic unity of the entire book." (2) "Implicit allusions to the second part of Isaiah in pre-exilic prophets sustain the Isaianic authorship." (3) "Unbroken tradition supports the Isaianic unity of the entire book." (4) "Evidence that the author of Isaiah 40-66 was a Palestinian favors Isaianic unity of the entire prophecy." (5) "Passages in 40-66 evidently pre-exilic in character, favor Isaianic unity."

Finally, Unger concludes by saying: ". . .Those who grant the supernatural in Biblical prophecy and comprehend the varied phenomena of its operation will find no valid reason to discard the traditional view of Isaianic authorship of the whole book in favor of modern views . . . ."[16]

The present writer appreciates the witness and dedication of those scholars in this ultra-conservative milieu, and must confess that he himself has gradually emerged out of some phases of this conservatism, but the evidence now appears to him to favor in many instances the modern critical positions. This is especially true where the literary composition of the Old Testament is concerned.[17]

### III.   Criteria of Delimitation

Modern critical scholarship has established, upon the basis of certain well-defined criteria, that the evidence requires the separation of Second Isaiah from the work of Isaiah of the eighth century. The present writer does not feel that it is necessary to defend this prevailing opinion, but he does feel that it would be well to list the principal criteria which have been adduced to prove that chapters 40-55 were penned by an author approximately two hundred years later than the eighth century. These criteria reflect a marked similarity, and are usually broken down into the following divisions: (1) historical situation; (2) literary style; (3) theological concepts.[18]

When one employs all these criteria and accumulates the overwhelming evidence in support of this prevailing opinion, he sees clearly the cardinal principle of Old Testament prophecy: that "the prophet addresses himself, at least primarily, to the situation of his own time." Indeed, it should be remembered that prophecy was never a magical but rather a moral institution. Hence, nothing would have been gained had the prophet enunciated his message to a people more than a century and one half before it was relevant and practicable.[19]

T. K. Cheyne agrees wholeheartedly with this view. In his own consideration of whether Isaiah of Jerusalem, a man with admitted exceptional gifts, could have projected himself two hundred years into the future,

Cheyne observes that this would have involved the prophet's assuming "not only the historical point of view, but even the linguistic peculiarities of a later age. . . ."[20] Certainly the farthest stretch of the imagination would hardly admit of this possibility.

## IV. Chapters 34-35

The evidence is rather conclusive that Isaiah 40-55 comes from a pen other than that of the Isaiah of the eighth century. But the question that now arises concerns chapters 34 and 35, which Torrey assigns also to the Second Isaiah.[21]

Bernhard Duhm, on the other hand, believes that both chapters 34 and 35 belong to a much later time. His judgment is based principally upon the apocalyptic or eschatological types which he discovers in these chapters.[22]

R. H. Pfeiffer considers Isaiah 34-35 a poetic unit in two parts. He observes that this poem is written in "dithyrambic and imaginative style," and that it resembles somewhat the style of Second Isaiah. It constitutes, he says, "an apocalyptic vision of Jehovah's final triumph."[23] Pfeiffer sees two acts in this drama: (1) chapter 34, the day of terrible vengeance upon Edom; (2) chapter 35, the terrestrial paradise, with blessings for Zion.[24]

Even though there are similarities between chapters 34-35 and Second Isaiah, Pfeiffer dates the former in the fifth century, and even possibly in the fourth. Thus, this poem, he concludes, could not be from the Second Isaiah.[25]

The present writer is in partial agreement with the critics mentioned above. He also doubts that chapter 34, a recognized eschatological poem with mythological allusions, can be attributed to the prophet of the Exile.[26] The principal reason for this writer's doubts is the eschatology reflected in the chapter. Although the element of judgment is certainly evident in Second Isaiah's eschatology, there is hardly anything there comparable to what is found in this poem. The judgment in chapter 34 is of tremendous scope, and includes the heavens, the earth, and all their host. "The description, cosmic in its sweep and perspective, is one of the most realistic, as it is one of the most appalling, in all Hebrew literature."[27]

It is, indeed, a poem of an apocalyptic nature, and with such lurid details, especially in its emphasis upon blood and slaughter (vv. 3, 4, 5-7), that one is reminded of the similar picture in Isaiah 63. In fact, there is such close affinity between the two portraits that this writer must assign them both to the post-exilic period.

When one turns to chapter 35, however, the picture is markedly different, and one has ample grounds, this author believes, for attributing this poem to the Second Isaiah. Many critics agree with this position. For instance, J. P. Hyatt says: "I believe that Deutero-Isaiah is the author of chapters 40-55 and probably also chapter 35."[28]

As early as 1915, A. T. Olmstead had set forth this same view. In commenting on chapters 36-39, Olmstead said that this material ". . .divides the body of the so-called Deutero-Isaiah, chapters 40f., from its introduction in chapter 35."[29]

In a later publication, Professor Olmstead cites the arguments in support of his position.[30] He argues that "87 per cent of the vocabulary of 35:1-9 is found in recognized work of II Isaiah. . . ." And, of course, all of verse 10 is repeated in Isaiah 51:11. Following a detailed analysis of Isaiah 35, and a comparison of its words with those found in Isaiah 40-55, Olmstead concludes that all of the words of the former, with the exception of fourteen, are discovered in the recognized portions of Second Isaiah. But the most important thing in this critic's thought is his claim that the majority of his words are "almost or quite peculiar to chapters 35 and 40-55."[31]

R. B. Y. Scott has made a very detailed study of Isaiah 35 in relation to Isaiah 40-55. His study has been based upon an examination of the vocabulary and word forms, style and usage, and subject matter. He concludes that the vocabulary evidence is indecisive, but the style and subject matter offer ". . .cumulative evidence. . .in favor of. . .adding chapter 35 to the authentic writings of Deutero-Isaiah."[32]

The preceding arguments for adding chapter 35 to the work of Second Isaiah are rather convincing. But in addition to these, the present writer would add another from his own study, namely, eschatology. This chapter clearly reflects the same eschatological motifs as are discovered in Second Isaiah: vv. 1-2, luxuriance of the desert; vv. 4-6a, reversal of present fortunes after Yahweh's advent; vv. 6b-7, water in the desert; vv. 8ff., the way through the desert; v. 10, eschatological singing.

E. J Kissane has observed that there is one vital difference between Isaiah 35 and chapters 40ff.  In Isaiah 40ff., "desert" is the way through which the exiles pass enroute to Palestine; but in chapter 35, the "desert" is Palestine itself.[33]

Upon the basis of all the evidence adduced above, the present author accepts Isaiah 35 as a part of Second Isaiah's work.  But since all the eschatological motifs in this chapter are duplicated in chapters 40-55, the present study will be confined to this latter block of materials whose authorship is generally unquestioned among critical scholars.

## V.  The Servant Passages

The Servant passages in Deutero-Isaiah have probably occasioned as much discussion as any other subject in Old Testament study.  But still the wealth of thought and literature has yet to yield any satisfactory unanimity of opinion, not only with reference to the identification of the "Servant" but also with reference to the authorship and actual identification of the poems themselves.

Since these Servant passages will not be dealt with in great detail in the subsequent chapters, the present writer desires to treat them a little more fully in this current discussion than would ordinarily be required.

Usually the Servant poems are identified as follows: (1) 42:1-4; (2) 49:1-6; (3) 50:4-9; (4) 52:13-53:12.[34] However, there are those critics whose identifications are different.  For example, C. C. Torrey extends the poems considerably.  He says: "The literary analysis which stops short at 42:4 without including vss. 6f., and at 49:6 without making vs. 8 an essential part of the same portrayal, merits profound suspicion."[35]   In addition, Torrey includes passages in Isaiah 61 and 62.[36]

Johannes Lindblom extends the first three Servant poems to include 42:1-9; 49:1-7; 50:4-11.[37] Sigmund Mowinckel extends the first and third poems, respectively, to 42:1-7 and to 50:4-11. However, he does have some misgivings about the last two verses (vv. 10-11) in the third poem.[38]

The question of the authorship of the Servant passages has been just about as involved as that of identification.   Duhm considered the Servant poems to be later than the time of Deutero-Isaiah and, of course, by another hand.[39]   Paul Volz accepted the first three as the work of the Second Isaiah, but argued that the fourth poem was probably from the pen of some author in the fourth or even third century B.C.[40]

Torrey has no problem with the question of authorship, since he holds to the unity of Isaiah 34-35, 40-66. He bases this judgment upon rhetoric, the prophet's imagination, and grammar and style.[41]

A number of other writers attribute the poems to Second Isaiah.[42]   Some of these scholars, however, hold that the Servant poems constitute an independent cycle of passages, and were, therefore, not an original part of the prophecy.   Levy maintains that these poems were later inserted into the general body of prophecies by Deutero-Isaiah himself.   Certain redactional verses were also added by the prophet to conceal the seams.[43] T. K. Cheyne agrees on this point. He holds that "a strict exegesis permits. . .no other conclusion than this . . .," namely, that the Servant poems are independent of their contexts. These poems were used, he says, by the prophet in the development of a theme when he needed a "stimulus for a fresh oratorical start. . . ."[44]

The most involved question of all concerning the Servant passages is the identification of the "Servant." C. R. North lists and discusses the four theories which he thinks now hold the field. They are (briefly) as follows:

1. The Servant identified with an anonymous contemporary of Second Isaiah. The prophet may have considered him to be the Messiah. This position may be labeled "historico-messianic."

2. The Servant identified with the prophet—the "autobiographical theory" (originated by Mowinckel).

3. The Servant identified with the corporate body—the "collective theory."

4. The Servant identified with the Messiah—the "Messianic theory."[45]

In addition to these, the present writer believes that other possibilities must be mentioned, just as North has done in a later publication.[46]

In this subsequent work, the following possible interpretations are given:

I. Jewish interpretations:

A. "Righteous" or "wise" of the community.
B. Messiah.
C. Jewish nation (general Jewish view).

II.  Christian interpretations:
     A. Isaiah 53—prophecy of Christ.
     B. Collective interpretations:
        1. Nation of Israel.
        2. Pious remnant of Israelites, or order of the prophets.
        3. Ideal—not historical Israel.
        4. Idea of corporate personality.
     C. Historical individual theories:
        1. Individual of the past.
        2. Anonymous contemporary of the prophet who, he believed, would be the Messiah.
        3. Autobiographical theory.

III. Mythological interpretations:
     A. Servant associated with the myth of the dying and rising God (Tammuz).

IV.  Messianic interpretations:
     A. Messianic king of the Davidic lineage.
     B. A soteriological rather than a royal figure.[47]

Although many suggestions have been made, some scholars attempt to identify the Servant rather precisely. For example, Mowinckel (in 1921) said pointedly that the suffering Servant was none other than the prophet Deutero-Isaiah himself.[48]  Sellin, at one juncture, identified the Servant as Jehoiakin, and still later as Moses.[49]  But, to say the least, such conjectures as these, even though they come from reputable scholars, are highly dubious. In fact, Karl Budde goes so far as to say that this "is nothing short of fantastic, and the extreme of absurdity."[50]  Muilenburg echoes the same

sentiments when he says that "no single person is suffi-
cient to bear the burden of what is disclosed in the
songs."[51]

Other interpretations of the Servant have laid stress
upon the corporate body. Exponents of this view have
been Otto Eissfeldt[52] and H. Wheeler Robinson.[53] In
developing his view, Eissfeldt explains that a group of
people (from the standpoint of Hebraic thought) was
more than just a collection of individuals. It was actually a psychical whole, and "in so far an ideal quantity
. . . ." Thus, when a Hebrew writer linked the term
"Ebed" with either Israel or Jacob it referred to the
"ideal and not the real entity. . . ." Robinson, on the
other hand, cites even the fluidity of this corporate concept. In the Songs the corporate personality is sometimes seen in the mass; sometimes it contracts to the
minority "in whom its mission is actually being realized"; or, finally, it may be "the one representative in
whose consciousness alone it actually exists at any given
moment of history. . . ."[54]

Lindblom offers the most unusual interpretation of
the Servant poems which this writer has discovered. In
his way of thinking the Servant is not to be identified
with any particular individual. The Servant poems are
to be interpreted allegorically or symbolically. In fact,
according to Lindblom, it is no more proper to ask who
the Servant is than to ask who the prodigal son is. The
proper question is: "What does the Suffering Servant
signify?" The answer is evident. Just as the prodigal
son represents the repentant people, so the Suffering
Servant signifies Israel in captivity.[55]

After all these views have been examined, and others considered,[56] it appears to this writer that some view similar to that expressed by J. P. Hyatt must be embraced:

> The Suffering Servant idea must include the nation Israel, but it is not exhausted by the national interpretation. It is an ideal which can be really fulfilled only in an individual, and to the Christian has been fulfilled in Jesus Christ.[57]

## VI.  Conclusions

From the foregoing considerations the writer draws the following conclusions with reference to the scope of this prophecy:

I.  The unity of the Book of Isaiah cannot be supported.

II.  The commonly used criteria—historical situation, literary style, and theological concepts—give adequate support to the view that chapters 40-55 belong to Deutero-Isaiah.

III.  The internal evidence in Isaiah 56-66 warrants the dating of this section later than chapters 40-55.  The similarities between the two sections may be attributed to any one of the three following reasons:

   A.  Chapters 56-66 were penned by disciples of Deutero-Isaiah.

   B.  Mechanical accident: Chapters 56-66, being placed in the same role with other passages from Isaiah as anonymous prophecies, gradually assumed the same name.

C. Conscious imitation.
IV. The evidence does not support Deutero-Isaiah's authorship of chapter 34, but there is overwhelming evidence for his authorship of chapter 35.
V. The study of Isaiah 40-55 fails to produce any strong evidence for denying the Servant passages to the prophet of the Exile.

Thus, since the eschatological motifs of chapter 35 are duplicated in the generally unquestioned section of Second Isaiah, the biblical basis for the development of the subsequent chapters will be Isaiah 40-55.

## NOTES AND REFERENCES

1. James Muilenburg, "Isaiah Chapters 40-66," *The Interpreter's Bible* (New York: Abingdon Press, 1956), V, 383; R. H. Pfeiffer, *Introduction to the Old Testament* (New York: Harper and Brothers Publishers, 1948), p. 415.

2. Muilenburg, *op. cit.*

3. D. Bernh. Duhm, *Das Buch Jesaia* ("Handkommentar zum Alten Testament"), ed., D. W. Nowack (Göttingen: Vandenhoeck und Ruprecht, 1892).

4. *Ibid.,* pp. XIII-XIV.

5. C. R. North, *Isaiah 40-55: Introduction and Commentary* (London: SCM Press Ltd., 1952), pp. 17, 18.

6. Otto Eissfeldt, *Einleitung in das Alte Testament* (Tübingen: J. C. B. Mohr [Paul Siebeck], 1934), pp. 388-389.

7. *Ibid.*

8. T. K. Cheyne, *Introduction to the Book of Isaiah* (London:

Adam and Charles Black, 1895), p. 238. Cf. also Reuben Levy, *Deutero-Isaiah: A Commentary* (London: Oxford University Press, 1925), p. 12.

9. North, *op. cit.,* pp. 17, 18.

10. Muilenburg, *op. cit.,* pp. 384, 414. Cf. also George Buchanan Gray's *A Critical Introduction to the Old Testament* (New York: Charles Scribner's Sons, 1913), pp. 184-186.

11. C. C. Torrey, *The Second Isaiah* (Edinburgh: T. & T. Clark, 1928).

12. *Ibid.,* pp. 7, 8.

13. Fleming James, *Personalities of the Old Testament* (New York: Charles Scribner's Sons, 1947), pp. 362-363; Torrey, *op. cit.,* pp. 50ff., 108, 109.

14. S. R. Driver, *An Introduction to the Literature of the Old Testament* (New York: Charles Scribner's Sons, 1894), p. 217. Others who share similar views are: W. A. L. Elmslie, *How Came Our Faith* (New York: Charles Scribner's Sons, 1949), pp. 339ff.; George Dahl, "Some Recent Interpretations of Second Isaiah," *JBL,* 48 (1929), pp. 362-377; Louis Finkelstein, *The Pharisees* (Philadelphia: The Jewish Publication Society of America, 1938), II, 627ff.

15. *Ibid.,* p. 628.

16. *Introductory Guide to the Old Testament* (Grand Rapids: Zondervan Publishing House, 1951), pp. 319-322.

17. In addition to Unger's work, cf. also B. A. Copass, *Isaiah: Prince of Old Testament Prophets* (Nashville: Broadman Press, 1944); Samuel A. Cartledge, *A Conservative Introduction to the Old Testament* (Grand Rapids: Zondervan Publishing House, 1943); *et al.*

18. John Edgar McFadyen, *Introduction to the Old Testament* (New York: George H. Doran Co., n.d.), pp. 129-130; S. R. Driver, *An Introduction to the Literature of the Old Testament* (New York: Charles Scribner's Sons, 1894), pp. 223-229.

19. McFadyen, *op. cit.,* p. 129.

20. Cheyne, *op. cit.,* p. 241.

21. Torrey, *op. cit.,* pp. 53-54.

22. Duhm, *op. cit.,* pp. XXI, 229-230. Cf. also James Muilenburg, "The Literary Character of Isaiah 34," *JBL,* LIX (1940) pp. 339-365.

23. Pfeiffer, *op. cit.,* p. 441.

24. *Ibid.*

25. *Ibid.*

26. Muilenburg, "The Literary Character of Isaiah 34," *op. cit.,* pp. 342ff.

27. *Ibid.,* p. 344.

28. J. P. Hyatt, *Prophetic Religion* (New York: Abingdon-Cokesbury Press, 1947), pp. 28-29.

29. A. T. Olmstead, "The Earliest Book of Kings," *AJSLL,* XXXI (1915), p. 196, note 4.

30. "II Isaiah and Isaiah, Chapter 35," *AJSLL,* LIII (1937), pp. 251-253.

31. *Ibid.;* but cf. Walter Harrelson, *Interpreting the Old Testament* (New York: Holt, Rinehart and Winston, Inc., 1964), p. 246.

32. R. B. Y. Scott, "The Relation of Isaiah, Chapter 35, to Deutero-Isaiah," *AJSLL,* LII (1936), pp. 178-191.

33. E. J. Kissane, *The Book of Isaiah* (Dublin: Browne and Nolan Ltd., 1941), I, 381.

34. Pfeiffer, *op. cit.,* p. 459; Ernest Sellin, *Introduction to the Old Testament,* trans. W. Montgomery (New York: George H. Doran Co., 1923), p. 143; Duhm, *op. cit.,* p. XIII; Otto Eissfeldt, "Ebed-Yahwe in Isaiah XL-LV in Light of Israelite Conceptions of Community and Individual," *The Expository Times,* XLIV (1932-33), pp. 261-268; North, *op. cit.,* p. 29.

35. Torrey, *op. cit.,* p. 148.

36. *Ibid.,* pp. 138-140.

37. Joh. Lindblom, *The Servant Songs in Deutero-Isaiah* (Lund: C. W. K. Gleerup, 1951), pp. 24-37.

38. S. Mowinckel, "Der Knecht Jahwäs," *Norsk Teologisk Tidsskrift,* II (1921), pp. 2-3. Cf. also Rowley, *The Servant of the Lord and Other Essays on the Old Testament* (London: Lutterworth Press, 1952), pp. 7ff.

39. Duhm, *op. cit.,* pp. XIII-XIV.

40. D. Paul Volz, *Jesaia II* (Kommentar zum Alten Testament), ed. Ernest Sellin (Leipzig: A. Deichert, 1932), IX, 189ff.; cf. also Lindblom, *op. cit.,* p. 13, note 3, who has presented a similar interpretation.

41. Torrey, *op. cit.,* p. 139.

42. James, *op. cit.,* p. 363; Sellin, *op. cit.,* p. 143; Eissfeldt, "Ebed-Yahwe in Isaiah XL-LV," p. 264; Muilenburg, *op. cit.,* p. 407.

43. Levy, *op. cit.,* pp. 13, 14.

44. Cheyne, *op. cit.,* p. 307. The supposition here is that the poems were written *prior* to the rest of the book. Still other views hold that the poems were composed by Second Isaiah *after* his book; or the poems were composed by an earlier author and then inserted by Second Isaiah, *et cetera.* Cf. Pfeiffer, *op. cit.,* pp. 459-462.

45. C. R. North, *The Suffering Servant in Deutero-Isaiah* (London: Oxford University Press, 1948), pp. 4-5.

46. North, *Isaiah 40-55.*

47. *Ibid.,* pp. 29-36.

48. Mowinckel, *op. cit.,* p. 9.

49. Sellin, *op. cit.,* pp. 143-144.

50. Karle Budde, "The So-Called 'Ebed-Yahweh Songs,' and the Meaning of the Term 'Servant of Yahweh' in Isaiah, Chaps. 40-55," *American Journal of Theology,* III (1899), p. 507.

51. Muilenburg, *op. cit.,* p. 9.

52. Eissfeldt, "Ebed-Yahwe in Israel XL-LV," pp. 267-268.

53. H. W. Robinson, *The Cross of the Servant: A Study in Deutero-Isaiah* (London: Student Christian Movement, 1926).

54. *Ibid.*, p. 83; cf. John Bright, *A History of Israel* (Philadelphia: The Westminster Press, 1959), pp. 340ff.; Harrelson, *op. cit.*, pp. 248ff.

55. Lindblom, *op. cit.*, p. 48.

56. Torrey, *op. cit.*, p. 138; George Adam Smith, *The Book of Isaiah* (New York: Doubleday, Doran & Co., Inc., 1927), II, 292; Edward J. Kissane, *The Book of Isaiah* (Dublin: Browne and Nolan, 1943), II, LXVIII.

57. Hyatt, *op. cit.*, p. 89. Cf. also Rowley, *op. cit.*, pp. 55-56, who is largely in agreement with Hyatt.

## Chapter 2

## THE HISTORY OF THE TIMES

### I. *The Immediate Background*

The history directly pertinent to this period begins with Nebuchadnezzar, king of Babylon, whose long and prosperous reign extended from 605 to 562 B.C.[1] The publication of five texts in the British Museum has thrown new light upon the reign of Nebuchadnezzar and the history of Judah in the period just prior to the fall of Jerusalem.[2] Hitherto the information on Nebuchadnezzar has been a little less specific than that which is now available. The extensive building operations of this king have, of course, long been known. Throughout his reign he concentrated upon the city of Babylon, in order to make his capital not only powerful and great but beautiful as well. The walls of this city were constructed with such painstaking care as to make the city practically impregnable. In addition to his work in Babylon, he rebuilt cities, repaired and erected temples, dug new canals and cleaned the old ones.[3]

The documents which have now been made available confirm the fact that there was a battle of Carchemish in 605 B.C., in which the Babylonians defeated the Egyptians. This battle is mentioned in Jeremiah 46:2 and by Josephus (*Ant. Jud.* X, vi, i; *Contra Apionem* I,

19).  B. M. 21946 *Obv.* lines 1-8 gives a rather full account of this engagement which, according to Wiseman, was in May-June, 605 B.C.[4]  Nebuchadnezzar, the crown prince and eldest son of Nabopolassar, was in command of the Babylonian army.  The record of this event claims a complete defeat of the Egyptian army. Moreover, it boasts that at the same time Nebuchadnezzar conquered the whole of Hatti (a general term for Syria-Palestine).  Wiseman admits that the Egyptian defeat was somewhat decisive but, at the same time, it is also recognized that the Egyptians still had enough strength to cause Nebuchadnezzar to make a number of invasions into Hatti to exercise his control there.[5]

Soon after the battle of Carchemish Nebuchadnezzar's father died, and the crown prince ascended the throne on the first of Elul (September 7, 605 B.C.).[6]  In the early part of his reign, Nebuchadnezzar's sovereignty over the smaller nations was recognized and accepted. In the kingdom of Judah, Jehoiakim—who had been placed on the throne by Pharaoh Necho of Egypt in place of this brother Jehoahaz—eventually made peace with the brilliant Babylonian monarch (II Kings 23:28-24:1; II Chronicles 36:6).  Three years later, however, he rebelled.  But when troops were dispatched by the Babylonians this revolt was soon quelled (II Kings 24:2).[7]

The texts from the British Museum throw new light upon Jehoiakim's revolt in 602/601 B.C.  Just as was indicated above, even after Carchemish the Egyptians still maintained strength and influence in Hatti, a fact that necessitated Nebuchadnezzar's making almost annual inroads into this area in order to maintain control and enforce the payment of tribute. It is now known that in the fourth year of Nebuchadnezzar's reign he came into direct conflict with the Egyptian army. The chronicle indicates that great destruction was inflicted upon both armies. In fact, it seems very likely from the Babylonian account that Nebuchadnezzar was defeated, for the next year the king remained at home and gathered together his chariots and horses in great numbers" (*Rev.* line 8).

It now appears obvious that this battle may have been precipitated by Jehoiakim's withholding tribute from Babylonia, and making an alliance with Egypt. Or, again, it has been suggested that Jehoiakim's change of allegiance came after he saw the success of Egypt. At any rate, the biblical account in II Kings 24:1, 2 (which seems to tie in nicely with the new data) says that "the Lord sent against him bands of the Chaldeans. . .Syrians . . .Moabites, and. . .Ammonites. . . ." In other words, Nebuchadnezzar sent marauding bands of his own men against this recalcitrant Judean King.

A second revolt broke out in Judah a few years later, which resulted in the first captivity of 597 B.C. The Babylonian Chronicle describes this event as follows:

> In the seventh year, month Kislev, the king of Akkad mustered his army and marched to Hatti; he encamped against the city of Judah..., and in the month Adar, second day, took the city and captured the king. He appointed in it a king after his own heart, received its heavy tribute, and sent it to Babylon.[8]

This account agrees generally with the Old Testament

accounts in II Kings 24:10-17; II Chronicles 36:10; and
Jeremiah 52:28.[9] The most significant fact derived from
this text is the precise date of this first captivity—the
second of Adar (March 16), 597 B.C.

All the available evidence supports the belief that
King Jehoiakim died before the city was actually taken,
and was succeeded by his eighteen-year-old son Jehoia-
chin, who reigned but three months before he surrendered to the Babylonians who were besieging the city
of Jerusalem (II Kings 24:10-12).[10] The youthful king,
along with his mother, members of his court, and a number of people in Judah, was bound with chains and taken
as a prisoner to Babylon, where he remained for thirty-
seven years.

When Jerusalem surrendered, Nebuchadnezzar appointed Zedekiah, another one of Josiah's sons, king of
Judah. Zedekiah ruled for eleven years (597-586 B.C.).
For ten years he pursued a pro-Babylonian policy, but
in 588 B.C. he yielded to pro-Egyptian pressure and
withheld tribute from Babylonia.[11] This brought Nebuchadnezzar's wrath upon the little kingdom of Judah.
Many of the towns were destroyed, and Jerusalem itself
was attacked. The city held out, however, for eighteen
months, but in 586 B.C., on the ninth of Ab, the
Babylonians entered the city.[12] Zedekiah was captured,
his eyes put out, and his sons slain (II Kings 25:2-7). In
addition, a great part of the city was burned, the walls
torn down, the temple and the royal palace virtually
destroyed, and a number of people exiled (vv. 8-11).
At this time Judah lost her independence, and became a
province of Babylonia, with a governor (Gedaliah)

instead of an independent king. Thus, the royal line of David had ceased. "A long chapter of history came to a close, and a new chapter opened."[13]

Although Jeremiah 52:30 states pointedly that only 4600 persons were carried into exile in all phases of the captivity,[14] general historical and archaelogical considerations lead some scholars to believe that there was a serious depletion of the population as a result of the deportations, as well as the semi-voluntary migrations, between the years 597 and 586 B.C. S. W. Baron is of the opinion that one-third of the total pre-war population of Judah was forcibly removed by the conqueror, while a great many others were killed or died of hunger and deprivation. This critic also believes that thousands of people fled the country before the Chaldean armies approached, and that only a part of them returned after peace was restored.[15]

W. F. Albright, one of the most eminent contemporary archaeologists, is in substantial agreement with the views expressed above. He says:

> The final Chaldean invasion of Judah almost completely denuded the central hill-country and the Shephelah of Judah, leaving Jewish settlers only in the Negeb..., and in the district to the north of Jerusalem which was under the control of the Babylonian governor of Samaria.[16]

After the conquest of Judah, Nebuchadnezzar continued to rule until 562 B.C., when he was succeeded by his son, Amel-Marduk (Evil-Merodach of II Kings 25: 27f.; Jeremiah 52:31-34). The latter's reign extended for merely two years (562-560 B.C.), at which time he was assassinated by his brother-in-law, whose name was Nergal-shar-usur, or Neriglissar (560-556 B.C.).[17]

According to Josephus (*Contra Apionem*, I, 20, 147), Amel-Marduk was a harsh ruler. He has also been described as one who "was restrained neither by law nor decency."[18] According to the Old Testament, however, he is pictured as generous toward the royal Judean captives (Jer. 52:31-34; II Kings 25:27-30).[19]

Amel-Marduk's successor, Neriglissar, has been described as a man of far stronger character than his predecessor.[20] He was the son of a private citizen, and had been an army commander under Nebuchadnezzar. In addition, he was married to a daughter of the same king. "Neriglissar is probably to be identified with Nergal-sharezer who held the office of *rab mag* at the siege of Jerusalem in 586 B.C. . . . ."[21]

One of the Babylonian chronicles (B. M. 25124) gives a new insight into the reign of Neriglissar. This tablet gives information for the year 557/556 B.C.—the third year of this king. It records the details of a military campaign which Neriglissar led into Cilicia.[22]

The son of Neriglissar, Labashi-Marduk, succeeded his father to the throne. But after a nine month's reign the youthful king was slain by a group of conspirators. Tradition says that this conspiracy was directed against the young king because he displayed evil traits of character.[23]

As soon as Labashi-Marduk was dead the conspirators chose a native Babylonian, who was not related to the reigning house, and placed him on the throne which had been filled the previous seventy years by Chaldeans.

This ruler was Nabu-naid, or Nabonidus (555-539 B.C.). Nabonidus was an extremely pious king whose interests centered around the building or restoration of religious temples. Coupled with these interests were his famous archaeological researches which he conducted particularly among the ruined palaces and temples. At the end of his reign Babylonia changed hands.[24]

Sidney Smith contends that the cuneiform documents are prejudiced against this last Babylonian king.[25] This prejudice stems particularly from the priests of Marduk, who wrote under the orders and in the interests of Cyrus, presumably to "reconcile the Babylonians to the loss of their independence by vilifying their last ruler."[26]

When the Assyrian Empire began to collapse in 612 B.C.,[27] with the fall of Nineveh, the Medes received the northern and eastern provinces. In 585 B.C. Cyaxares, king of the Medes, stretched his frontier farther to the west. This action resulted from the defeat of the Urartu kingdom. The river Halys then became the boundary between the Medes and the Lydians.

Astyages, son of Cyaxares, succeeded to the Median throne and reigned until 550 B.C., at which time he was defeated by Cyrus, the rising Persian prince. Hitherto Cyrus had been king of Anshan, a Persian province in Elam, since assuming his father's throne in 559 B.C. A. T. Olmstead contends that this contest between Cyrus and his suzerain was precipitated by the former's rebellion against Media after Nabonidus had entered into an alliance with him.[28] In this engagement Astyages' army mutinied, seized its king, and turned him over to Cyrus. Ecbatana was captured, and its treasures carried to Anshan.

This victory now gave Cyrus control of a tremendous kingdom. Indeed, "no king of any Oriental people had ever before ruled a dominion so vast or so rich."[29]

Thus, it is not surprising that the neighboring peoples were startled and frightened by this rising conqueror. Accordingly, in 547 B.C. a coalition was formed against Cyrus, consisting of Croesus of Lydia, Amasis of Egypt, and Nabu-naid of Babylonia who, by this time, had broken off his alliance with Cyrus. In an additional effort to ward off this conqueror whose territory already practically touched his, Croesus secured from Sparta the promise of her fleet to assist in this campaign against Cyrus.[30]

Cyrus somehow learned of the plan of his enemies, and attacked Croesus of Lydia before the latter's allies could come to his aid. In this first battle the Persians scored an indecisive victory, but in the second battle Croesus was driven from the field in a hopeless rout. He then retired to Sardis, his capital city, in the belief that Cyrus would not pursue because of the approaching winter weather. Cyrus, however, had no intentions of allowing his enemy time for reinforcements, and attacked despite adverse conditions. After a fourteen-day siege the "supposedly impregnable acropolis of Sardis was scaled and Croesus made prisoner (547)."[31] This victory was followed by an assault upon the Greek city-states of Caria and Lydia within the next three years.[32]

After scoring these decisive victories, Cyrus placed one of his generals in charge of his western campaign and turned in person to the subjection of Babylonia. The way for this new campaign was not only paved by Cyrus' genius, but also by the ineffectiveness of the Babylonian king, Nabonidus, who displayed neither zeal for war nor yet for civil administration, but only for religion. Moreover, Nabonidus seems to have lived away from Babylon most of the time, at Tema. During his prolonged absences, he would leave the affairs of state to his son Belshazzar.[33] As a consequence of this general neglect, the disaffected elements in the population increased, especially among the priesthood of Marduk. Rogers suggests that Second Isaiah's prophecies (45:1-4; 46:1, 2; 47:1-5) also helped to weaken the people's faith in Nabonidus.[34]

Thus, near the beginning of October, in the year 539 B.C., Cyrus earned a decisive victory over the Babylonians at Opis, on the Tigris, and burned the people with fire. Bel-shar-usur (Belshazzar), son of Nabonidus, was the defeated general in this battle. Subsequently, Cyrus' opponents lost courage, and Sippar was taken without a battle on October 11. Two days later, Gobryas, governor of Gutium, whom Cyrus had placed over Assyria, entered Babylon without a battle. This was on October 13, 539 B.C.[35] Nabonidus fled to Borsippa, while Belshazzar perished in the city's fall.[36] A little over two weeks later (October 29), Cyrus made a triumphal entrance into the city, at which time he offered worship to Marduk, the chief god of this metropolis.[37] In keeping with Cyrus' generally lenient policy toward those he conquered, the city received tremendous consideration from the victors. The temples were carefully guarded against profanation and the customary looting.

It should be remembered, however, that when Cyrus entered Babylon he inaugurated a program of propagan-

da against the memory of the former Babylonian rulers—
Nabonidus and Belshazzar.   By attributing to them
religious laxity, he tried to show why their gods had
forsaken them.   Conversely, he endeavored to show how
he himself, the righteous prince, was the personal choice
of Marduk.  As evidence of his choice, Marduk supposedly directed Cyrus to Babylon, and without conflict or
battle gave him the city.  The Cyrus Cylinder makes the
following assertions:

> ...He made him set out on the road to Babylon...going
> at his side like a real friend.... Without any battle, he made
> him enter his town Babylon...,sparing Babylon...any calam-
> ity.   He delivered into his hands Nabonidus, the king who
> did not worship him (i.e. Marduk).[38]

In addition to the historical data which have been
given above, Sidney Smith argues that there are some
unrecognized historical materials in chapters 40-55 of
Isaiah.  His entire effort is aimed at getting back to the
"contemporary meaning" of the prophecies, to the facts
allegedly overlooked by the modern interpreters.  For
instance, in Isaiah 41:1-7 Smith sees not only a reference to Cyrus, the one who is raised up from the east,
but he also finds a reference to the Lydians, who are
probably the unnamed foes.  There is also here a prob-
able reference to the speed which Cyrus employed when
he marched to Sardis from the Halys.  The reference in
Isaiah 41:3 to Cyrus' pursuing "them" and passing on
safely or in peace is a possible allusion to the Lydian
army's not opposing the Persian advance.[39]

In the first Servant passage (42:1-4), Smith finds three
affirmations about the Persian king: (1) He will impose

judgment on the heathen nations. (2) He will not call up levies for military service in the subject provinces. (3) He will not abandon the western lands. These affirmations were probably necessary because some were wondering whether a foreign king would interest himself in the affairs of Palestine. Thus, this affirmation of Yahweh by His prophet was calculated to dispel doubts about Cyrus.[40]

It is, of course, possible, just as Smith contends upon the basis of Isaiah 45:1-7, that the prophet actually witnessed the fall of Babylon, and in this section describes the custom of forcing captured kings to open and shut the great gates as commanded. The picture here is obviously of their opening the gates to the victorious Cyrus (v. 1).[41]

Shortly after Cyrus had completed his first year as king of Babylon, he retired to his summer home in Ecbatana, and from there issued his famous edict (Ezra 6:3-5; cf. 5:14-16 and chapter 1) which permitted the Jewish exiles to return to their homeland to rebuild their devastated temple. In addition, they were permitted to return the gold and silver utensils of the Lord's house, which Nebuchadnezzar had taken and brought to Babylon.[42]

The historicity and authenticity of this edict has been sharply debated. C. C. Torrey has been one of the strongest opponents of its authenticity,[43] but in this he has by no means stood alone.[44] On the other hand, however, just as competent scholars argue for its authenticity. James Muilenburg, for instance, observes that the available accounts portray Cyrus as a benevolent sovereign, although, as this critic notices, the accounts do "betray a propagandistic penchant." Nevertheless, Muilenburg says: ". . .the edict of Cyrus. . .has doubtless a historical basis."[45]   W. F. Albright agrees: "The substantial historicity of the Edict of Cyrus in 538. . .has been confirmed by modern archaeological discoveries . . . ."[46]

Until more convincing evidence is adduced by those who attack its authenticity, the present writer shares the view that the Cyrus edict has some historical basis, and that there was, accordingly, an actual restoration, just as is anticipated in Second Isaiah and indicated in Ezra-Nehemiah.

## II.   The Influence of the Historical Conditions
## on Second Isaiah's Thought

It is the present writer's conviction that Second Isaiah's prophecies are intimately related to the historical context—to the needs and problems of the people he was addressing.   Contemporary writers likewise agree with this position.   C. R. North, for instance, says that "it is a cardinal principle that the Old Testament prophets related their prophecies to concrete and particular situations. . . ."[47]   Certainly it is not to be expected that a prophet as eminent as the Second Isaiah would do otherwise.   W. B. Stevenson assumes also that the contents and character of Deutero-Isaiah's public utterances were chiefly determined by the particular circumstances to which they were addressed, "so that the successive stages of his career are necessarily to some extent reflected in them. . . ."[48]

In the light of the historical conditions which faced the Jewish people during the Exile, the role played by Second Isaiah assumes an even greater status. Some critics have conjectured that the prophet was one of Cyrus' courtiers, and that some of his utterances may be compositions written in honor of the conqueror (41:1-13, 21-28; 42:5-9; 43:1-8; 44:24-28; 45:1-8, 9-13; 46:1-13; 48:12-16).[49]

Again, it has been conjectured (and with more cogency, in the thinking of the present writer) that the prophet was the spiritual leader of the Exile. Accordingly, when the exiles gathered on the Sabbath, Second Isaiah came and preached to his people messages of comfort, hope, and instruction.[50] In any event, the exigencies of the time made the role of this man of God a very significant one. Perplexing problems confronted his people, and made the prophet all the more anxious to provide some rational clues to their current dilemma.

Henry Sloane Coffin summarizes quite pointedly some of the religious perplexities among the devout exiles:

> The destruction of Jerusalem and the captivity in Babylon had been recognized as punishment for national sin. But not all Israelites had been equally sinful.... The misery of the loyally devout appeared to reflect upon the faithfulness and justice of God. Did he forget and neglect his people? Had he given up his purpose, announced to their forefathers, of making their seed a blessing to mankind? They looked at imposing images of Gods of force. Could it be that their God was less mighty and unable to deliver his worshipers?... They felt themselves a doomed people, with an uncaring or perhaps an incapable deity.[51]

The prophet's task was, indeed, more than the mere issuing of an announcement of Israel's forthcoming deliverance. He has to explain the significance of the Exile in God's plan for Israel and for the world, and why Yahweh has now resolved to intervene in Israel's behalf. This necessitates his dealing with Israel's special relationship to Yahweh, the reason for the unhappy interlude, and the necessity for the resumption of that pleasant association which Israel had previously enjoyed with her God.[52]

The prophet has to explain that God chose Israel in the person of Abraham to effect a definite purpose, namely, to make the true God known to all men (49:6). Thus Israel was under Yahweh's special care, but because of her sins chastisement had to be inflicted in the form of the Exile. The Exile would not only punish Israel for its apostasy, but would purge the nation of its wicked elements and leave a righteous remnant.

Thus, God's original purpose remained intact, even though apparently frustrated by the Exile. But the Exile could not endure permanently. Now that Israel's sins had been expiated, the time for deliverance had come.[53]

Second Isaiah was particularly stirred to prophecy when he noticed the meteoric rise of Cyrus to power. He detected in this brilliant conqueror the one chosen by Yahweh to liberate His people. The prophet's task was clear-cut: he must prepare the people to embrace freedom when the time and opportunity arose. But this was to be no easy task. It would involve the creation of a new state of mind among the people in Exile, for some had manifestly lost hope of a return and had decided to accept the inevitable, and thus to make the most of their current plight. Out of this context the prophet's message emerged.[54]

The reader of Second Isaiah's prophecies notes immediately an atmosphere markedly different from that of the earlier prophets. In place of harsh rebukes and announcements of impending doom, one finds hope and encouragement—even a future that is bright with promise. With rising crescendo this mood of hope is buttressed by "a remarkable argument demonstrating the power of God as seen in the mighty works of nature, and his supremacy over all the world. Nowhere is the omnipotence of Yahweh more eloquently or powerfully presented than by this unknown prophet." This was, of course, necessary because some of the exiles had developed doubts about Yahweh's ability to care for them, since He had apparently succumbed to the greater power of the Babylonian gods.[55] To counteract these doubts, the prophet tells in glowing words of God's supremacy, omnipotence, and solicitous care for his homeless children (cf. 40:9-11, 12-20, 21-23; 41:18-20; 45:20f.).

It is apparent from the prophecies of Second Isaiah that the exiles were often confronted with the vexing problem of Yahweh's relation to other gods. During these times the Israelites were brought face to face with the heathen world in a singular way. Heathen deities surrounded them on every hand. They were confronted also with an imposing heathen culture. Thus, in the presence of this extremely seductive environment, if they were to retain their faith in Yahweh, it was imperative that they be reminded again and again that He

alone was God. Consequently, the great prophet recurs
to this thought time and time again. He says: "I am the
Lord, and there is no other, besides me there is no God"
(45:5). "Before me no god was formed, nor shall there
be any after me. I, I am the Lord, and besides me
there is no savior" (43:10-11). "And there is no other
god besides me, a righteous God and a Savior; there is
none besides me" (45:21).[56]

In adducing his most convincing argument, Second
Isaiah starts from God's creative activity. This becomes
the decisive evidence for His unique divine power. Indeed, all the nations are but a drop from a bucket to
Him (40:15). Over against Him stand the impotent idol
gods. Even though made of wood and *covered with
gold,* they nevertheless represent nothing more than the
work of men (44:9-20), unworthy even of being mentioned in the same breath with the almighty, everlasting
God of Israel.[57]  Moreover, these much-adored idols of
Babylon were soon to fall, and in any event they were
unable to prevent Israel's release, which her own great
God would shortly effect.[58]

This great God whose creative handiwork reflects
such magnitude and grandeur that it defies human imagination (44:24; 45:12, 18; 48:13; 51:13; 54:16), is in
complete control of this universe, and all nations and
peoples are subject to him. In speaking of the emphasis which Second Isaiah placed upon the creatorship of
God, A. C. Knudson emphasizes the measure of comfort that would arise from the people's realizing "that
the covenant-God of Israel was none other than the
creator of heaven and earth. . . ."[59]

Second Isaiah teaches also that this creator God is the director of all human history. In fact, the recent victories of Cyrus proved this fact (41:2ff., 25; 43:12), and revealed as well that God was about to redeem Israel. Indeed, this very action in history would show to the whole world that He alone was God, and had the power to do all that He had foretold (42:5-8; 41:21-29; 42:9; 43:9, 10, 12; 48:14; 46:9-10).

All of the speeches in Second Isaiah are really intended to show that God still loves His people and that their chastisement had been for their sins (50:1; 43:27f.; 48:1f.), but God's grace and forgiveness have now been extended (40:2; 43:25; 44:22), and Israel is soon to discover again the purpose that the creator has for her. Indeed, God will now assert Himself and gain renown over all the earth by restoring His people to their homeland. This will not result from efforts exerted by the idols, but from the direction and power of Yahweh who actually decreed and then predicted it through His prophets.[60] In fact, the prophet challenges the idol gods to bring forward any proofs that they have taken an active part in the events; but, of course, they have nothing to show (44:7b; 45:21; 48:14; 41:21-24).

Reuben Levy observes:

> From the thought of a renascence of Israel, the prophet leads on to his teaching concerning the special function in the world of this renewed Israel, as the agent of God to the nations.... It was, however, the unknown prophet of the Exile who first consistently and clearly declared that Israel was to be a 'light to the nations' and was to lead them to a knowledge of God, which he (Israel) alone

as yet possessed. He was to show, with what must have seemed 'divine folly' at the time, that Israel, though crushed and miserable, hidden away in holes, blind and deaf, and feeling that God had forsaken him, was yet to be proof of Yahweh's might and sole Godhead.[61]

Levy has indeed touched upon a significant facet of Second Isaiah's prophecy. Even though the people were in the midst of their captivity, with all the accompanying miseries, the prophet's faith in God and certainty of the realization of Israel's purpose never dimmed. It is remarkable that the prophet *never* wearies of describing the glories which God will shortly effect for His people. Righteousness, honor, peace, and happiness will flourish, all under the rule and reign of God Himself (45:17; 46:13; 48:18f.; 49:8-50:3; 51:1f.).[62]

The apparent incongruity of the prophet's beatific portrait is brought into much sharper focus when one reflects upon the *actual* conditions of the Israelites during their exile. It is of course true, just as some writers have indicated, that "not all Jews in Babylonia were anti-Babylonian."[63] Thus, for some, the sad lament of Psalm 137 was hardly appropriate; but, at the same time, according to the evidence in Second Isaiah, many of the less prosperous exiles had ample grounds for despair and heavy hearts.

According to Isaiah 54:3; 49:8; and 49:19, Israel had suffered a severe devastation. For the prophet speaks of the "desolate cities," the "desolate heritages," and "your waste and your desolate places and your devastated land." Since "devastation and destruction, famine and sword" (51:18-20) had struck, the people were genuinely in need of an inspiring and encouraging message.

In addition, there had been a widespread scattering of the people since the days of Tiglath-pileser in 733 B.C. Subsequent deportations had followed in the days of Sargon and Sennacherib (722 and 701 B.C.), and much more recently in 597 and 586 B.C. by the Chaldeans. According to Amos 1:6, 9, slave raids had also accounted for many individual's being in remote lands. Added to this number were those who had been sold into slavery, perhaps to some foreigner (Neh. 5:8), because of indebtedness. Of course, as is usually true, some Israelites had migrated voluntarily, possibly to escape war and famine (Jer. 42:14), or possibly for commercial reasons. At any rate, Second Isaiah sees this widespread scattering as a "monstrous abnormality, an unmitigated calamity, to be rectified only by the reassembling of all dispersed Israelites in the home-land."[64]

According to Second Isaiah, the scattered Israelites were in trying circumstances. Probably what he says applies largely to those in Babylonia, the chief hardship being simply the Exile itself (cf. 45:13). But still there seems to have been more. Even though the prophet uses figures of speech freely, the exiles must still have been the recipients of oppression and ill treatment; for the prophet says pointedly:

> But this is a people robbed and plundered,
>    they are all of them trapped in holes
>    and hidden in prisons;
> they have become a prey with none to rescue,
>    a spoil with none to say, "Restore!"[65]

Again, he says:

> I was angry with my people,
>   I profaned my heritage;
> I gave them into your hand,
>   you showed them no mercy;
> On the aged you made your yoke
>   exceedingly heavy.[66]

It has been suggested that even where the Jews were unmolested by the government, adequate protection was not given to them. The general attitude toward them seems to have been rather hostile, according to the prophet. In 41:11 Second Isaiah speaks of "all who are incensed against you," and of "those who strive against you." In 54:15 he speaks of "whoever stirs up strife with you." But perhaps the hardest thing the exiles had to bear was the contempt with which they were held in some circles. In 51:7 the prophet exhorts the people: "fear not the reproach of men, and be not dismayed at their revilings." Thus, it was not necessarily blows but taunts which stung just as sharply.[67]

All of this naturally had an effect upon the mind of Israel. Instead of bringing out their courage and their faith in God it did just the opposite. Some actually turned against Him, with the feeling that He had cast them off. Because of this attitude, the prophet chided them, as is indicated in 40:27. Again, others went so far as to think that Yahweh was played out, that He had become faint and weary (40:28). Still others became defiant and angry (45:24; 45:9; 46:12; 48:4), alleging that His ancient power to deliver and sustain His people had not proved equal to the new time with its greater needs (50:2).[68]

As a result of the charges brought against Yahweh, some of the despairing people turned and took refuge in idolatry.[69]   The prophet's vehement attacks upon the folly of idolatry give convincing evidence that it was practiced widely among the Israelites.   Indeed, there seems to have been those who, when fortune smiled upon them, were ready to attribute such to their idol (48:5).

This picture of conditions among the exiles does not seem in any way to have depressed the great unknown prophet.   Rather, it seems to have elated him, for he saw in this a call for God to intervene.   Eventually the heavenly command did come to him to speak words of encouragement and hope to the downtrodden people (40:6ff.), and to tell them what God had purposed, and would shortly do in their behalf.   It was of course true that Israel could not go without rebuke, but the primary need, just as the prophet detected, was not for upbraiding but for the restoring of confidence and hope.   Israel "had lost heart, lost belief in its God and in its destiny."   Thus "comfort" was now wanted and needed.   This the prophet could (and did) give, "for he possessed it in overflowing measure."[70]

It is now clear, the present writer believes, just as has been shown above, that Second Isaiah addressed himself to the needs of his people, all of which had arisen within the particular historical context.   A quick, sweeping survey of chapters 40-55 will reveal how the motif of encouragement and hope obtains throughout his whole work.   Chapter 40 reminds the people that God's purpose cannot be frustrated by pagan gods nor by the power of man. Chapters 41:1-42:4 give assurance that just as the promises were fulfilled to Abraham in the conquest of Canaan, so the promise of deliverance made to Israel will be fulfilled. Chapters 42:5-43:13 promise that the New Exodus will be a type of the historical Exodus. The present plight is but chastisement for their sins, but the chastisement is now at an end. For the God who overthrew the Egyptians at the Sea of Reeds has likewise decreed the overthrow of Babylon (43:14-17). Indeed, the One who chose Israel is now coming to her aid (43:26-44:5). Israel need not fear the gods of Babylon, for they are merely the work of men's hands (44:6-23). God has promised victory to Cyrus, the one who will bring liberation to Israel. Through this restoration people will recognize the supremacy of Yahweh, and will know that all other gods are powerless. The gods of Babylon are surely powerless to save their people (ch. 46), for they, like Babylon herself, will be taken captive (ch. 47). When Israel disobeyed God's law, she was threatened with chastisement; this chastisement came, the pledge that the promised deliverance will also come (ch. 48).

Chapters 49-55 are certainly calculated to "rouse the nation in exile from its state of despondency" because they dwell on the "glories of the future, which include the national revival in a rebuilt and restored Zion...."[71]

### III. Summary

The historical background for this prophecy is of particular significance because the principal themes emerged directly out of the historical situation, in an attempt to meet the needs of the people of the Exile. These themes, it is true, were not altogether novel, but they were timely and carefully developed. For the prophet realized that if his message of hope and encouragement was to be effective in offsetting the pageantry, splendor, and color of the Babylonian cult, there would have to be a kind of competing pageantry, one of eschatological dimensions. But this was, by no means, a mere literary device! It stemmed from his own theological hopes— nay, expectations, which would be realized in the final events of history, on the brink of which he and his people then stood.

In the meantime—even before God's kingdom came in all its fullness—there was to be a kind of "realized eschatology," the prelude to that which would shortly be experienced in perfect splendor and glory. Thus, the only possible way to express the hope which he had, and which he wished to communicate to his downtrodden people, was through the medium of eschatological language and categories, just as we shall explain in our subsequent treatment.

But before we treat thoroughly of the prophet's eschatology, we want to look briefly at some of his other ideas, which we shall do in the following chapter.

## NOTES AND REFERENCES

1. R. A. Parker and W. H. Dubberstein, *Babylonian Chronology, 626 B.C.-45 A.D.* (Chicago: The University of Chicago Press, 1942), p. 10.

2. D. J. Wiseman, *Chronicles of Chaldean Kings (626-556 B.C.) in the British Museum* (London: The Trustees of the British Museum, 1956).

3. Robert W. Rogers, *A History of Babylonia and Assyria* (New York: Eaton & Mains, 1900), II, 316ff.; 343ff.

4. Wiseman, *op. cit.*, p. 25.

5. *Ibid.*, pp. 23, 24.

6. *Ibid.*, pp. 26, 27.

7. H. P. Smith, *Old Testament History* (New York: Charles Scribner's Sons, 1906), p. 283; Rogers, *op. cit.*, p. 318.

8. B.M. 21946 *Rev.* lines 11-13.

9. The difficulties occasioned by this account, as well as the discrepancies among the biblical accounts, are discussed by J. P. Hyatt in his "New Light on Nebuchadnezzar and Judean History," *JBL*, LXXV (1956), pp. 277-284.

10. Wiseman, *op. cit.*, p. 33.

11. Rogers, *op. cit.*, pp. 320ff.; J. P. Hyatt, "Jeremiah," *The Interpreter's Bible* (New York: Abingdon Press, 1956), V, 778.

12. II Kings 25:3ff.; cf. also Rogers, *op. cit.*, p. 329; James Muilenburg, "Isaiah 40-66," *The Interpreter's Bible*, V, 394.

13. Muilenburg, *op. cit.*, p. 395.

14. Cf. Hyatt, "Jeremiah," *op. cit.*, p. 1141.

15. S. W. Baron, *A Social and Religious History of the Jews* (New York: Columbia University Press, 1952), I, 105-106; cf. Rogers, *op. cit.*, p. 332.

16. W. F. Albright, *From the Stone Age to Christianity* (Baltimore: The Johns Hopkins Press, 1940), pp. 246-247.

17. Parker and Dubberstein, *op. cit.*, p. 10.

18. Leonard W. King, *A History of Babylon* (New York: Frederick A. Stokes Company, n.d.), II, 280.

19. Wiseman, *op. cit.*, p. 38.

20. King, *loc. cit.*

21. Wiseman, *loc cit.;* cf. also Jer. 39:3, 13.

22. *Ibid.,* p. 39.

23. Rogers, *op. cit.,* p. 358.

24. *Ibid.,* p. 360; for details of Nabonidus' reign cf. A. T. Olmstead, *History of Palestine and Syria* (New York: Charles Scribner's Sons, 1931), pp. 545-547; Sidney Smith, *Isaiah: Chapters XL-LV* (London: Oxford University Press, 1944), pp. 24-26.

25. Cf. the so-called Nabonidus Chronicle in *Ancient Near Eastern Texts,* ed. James B. Pritchard (Princeton: Princeton University Press, 1955), pp. 305-307.

26. Sidney Smith, *Isaiah: Chapters XL-LV,* p. 30.

27. Cf. the Babylonian Chroncile, No. 21, 901, in Pritchard, *op. cit.,* pp. 303-305, which describes the capture of Nineveh.

28. Olmstead, *History of the Persian Empire* (Chicago: The University of Chicago Press, 1948), p. 36.

29. Rogers, *A History of Ancient Persia* (New York: Charles Scribner's Sons, 1929), p. 39.

30. *Ibid.,* pp. 40ff.

31. Olmstead, *History of the Persian Empire, op. cit.,* p. 40.

32. *Ibid.,* pp. 41-44; J. M. P. Smith, *The Prophets and Their Times* (Chicago: The University of Chicago Press, 1940), p. 218.

33. Rogers, *A History of Ancient Persia, op. cit.,* pp. 56-57; Olmstead, *History of the Persian Empire, op. cit.,* p. 45, says that "Babylonia had progressively disintegrated under the weakling rule of Belshazzar."

34. *Ibid.,* pp. 58-60; Olmstead, *History of Palestine and Syria, op. cit.,* p. 551, conjectures that Second Isaiah's predictions cheered and inspired Cyrus in his victorious campaign against Babylonia.

35. Olmstead, *History of the Persian Empire, op. cit.,* p. 50.

36. Rogers, *A History of Ancient Persia, op. cit.,* p. 62.

37. *Ibid.;* J. M. P. Smith, *The Prophets and Their Times, op. cit.,* p. 219, says that the citadel in Babylon offered some re-

sistance and did not surrender to the Persians until March of 538 B.C.

38. James B. Pritchard, ed., *Ancient Near Eastern Texts* (Princeton: Princeton University Press, 1955), pp. 315-316.

39. Sidney Smith, *Isaiah: Chapters XL-LV*, pp. 49-50.

40. *Ibid.,* pp. 54-57.

41. *Ibid.,* pp. 72-73.

42. Olmstead, *History of Palestine and Syria, op. cit.,* p. 556.

43. C. C. Torrey, *The Second Isaiah* (Edinburgh: T. & T. Clark, 1928), p. 17; "The Composition and Historical Value of Ezra-Nehemiah," *Beihefte zur Zeitschrift für die alttestamentliche Wissenschaft,* II (1896), pp. 1-65.

44. H. P. Smith, *Old Testament History, op. cit.,* pp. 344ff., cites several reasons for holding to this position.

45. Muilenburg, *op. cit.,* p. 396 and n. 51.

46. W. F. Albright, "A Brief History of Judah from the Days of Josiah to Alexander the Great," *The Biblical Archaeologist,* IX (Feb., 1946), pp. 2-16; John Bright, *A History of Israel* (Philadelphia: The Westminster Press, 1959), pp. 342-343.

47. C. R. North, "The Interpretation of Deutero-Isaiah," *Norsk Teologisk Tidsskrift,* 1-2, Hefte (1955), p. 136.

48. W. B. Stevenson, "Successive Phases in the Career of the Babylonian Isaiah," *Werden und Wesen des Alten Testaments (Beih. z. ZAW), LXVI* (1936), p. 89.

49. Muilenburg, *op. cit.,* pp. 397-398; Reuben Levy, *Deutero-Isaiah: A Commentary* (London: Oxford University Press, 1925), p. 7.

50. Muilenburg, *op. cit.,* p. 398; Abraham J. Heschel, *The Prophets* (New York: Harper & Row, Publishers, 1962), p. 152.

51. Henry Sloane Coffin, "Exposition of Isaiah 40-66," *The Interpreter's Bible,* V, 420; cf. also Ulrich E. Simon, *A Theology of Salvation* (London: S.P.C.K., 1953), pp. 2-3.

52. Edward J. Kissane, *The Book of Isaiah* (Dublin: Browne

and Nolan, Ltd., 1943), II, XXXIV.

53. *Ibid.;* S. R. Driver, *Isaiah: His Life and Times* (New York: A. D. F. Randolph & Company, n.d.), pp. 168-169.

54. J. M. P. Smith, *op. cit.,* p. 220.

55. *Ibid.;* R. Levy, *Deutero-Isaiah: A Commentary* (London: Oxford University Press, 1925), p. 18.

56. A. C. Knudson, *The Religious Teaching of the Old Testament* (New York: The Abingdon Press, 1918), pp. 89, 90.

57. Johs. Pedersen, *Israel: Its Life and Culture* (London: Oxford University Press, 1940), III-IV, 599.

58. Levy, *op. cit.,* p. 19.

59. Knudson, *op. cit.,* pp. 124, 125.

60. Pedersen, *op. cit.,* p. 600.

61. Levy, *op. cit.,* p. 20.

62. Pedersen, *op. cit.,* p. 602.

63. Cf. especially the very realistic portrait of exilic conditions given by Baron, *op. cit.,* p. 115.

64. Fleming James, *Personalities of the Old Testament* (New York: Charles Scribner's Sons, 1947), pp. 365-366.

65. Isaiah 42:22.

66. Isaiah 47:6.

67. James, *op. cit.,* p. 367.

68. *Ibid.*

69. W. O. E. Oesterley and T. H. Robinson, *Hebrew Religion: Its Origin and Development* (New York: The Macmillan Company, 1930), p. 229.

70. *Ibid.,* p. 368; Driver, *op. cit.,* pp. 169-170.

71. Kissane, *op. cit.,* pp. XXXVI-XXXIX.

*Chapter 3*

## THEOLOGICAL IDEAS

With the background we have provided (scope and history), we need now to look at some of the significant theological ideas enunciated by our prophet, such as God, covenant, and sin. We shall, however, reserve the treatment of Isaiah's doctrine of salvation for our closing chapter—a doctrine which will become patent in the subsequent interpretation of the prophecy.

### I. God

Second Isaiah has one of the most advanced concepts of God to be found in the Old Testament. Before we set forth his "doctrine" of God, however, it would be well to note that the Old Testament hardly lays claim to any systematized teaching on this subject.

Walther Eichrodt has well reminded us that formal instruction about the being of God or His attributes are nowhere to be found in Holy Writ. The Israelite's knowledge of God came to him from his actual experience of the Deity, from the events of history, as they were interpreted by the spiritual leaders of the time. Thus, the awareness of God stemmed not from abstract concepts but from personal experience or encounter.[1]

### 1. His Nature

There are several designations for the Deity in the Old Testament, but the name employed by Second Isaiah is the name typically associated with Moses and the Sinai covenant.[2] For our prophet, however, the name Yahweh is associated especially with the idea of eternity. God is the First and the Last. Before Him no being was created and after Him nothing will exist (Isaiah 40:28; 41:4; 43:10f.; 44:6; 48:12).

Second Isaiah, it should be noticed, is the first prophet to connect creation with eternity. Since He created all that is, He stands above all that He has made, including time itself. In fact, He not only brings all things into existence, He is present and active in the *eschaton*—even to bring His purpose to pass.

The Kingship of Yahweh is particularly emphasized in Second Isaiah, for it is He who brings in the new age, in which all the nations of the earth will acknowledge His lordship (52:7, 10). Indeed, Yahweh proves that He is King of Israel for He liberates His own people, and through them effects salvation for all the nations. This accent upon Yahweh's lordship provides the Israelites with a much-needed spiritual lift because it negated the claims and pretensions of the "great king" and sovereign of this world under whom they had been forced to live.

### a. God's Oneness

Second Isaiah lays particularly strong emphasis on Yahweh's oneness (41:29; 43:10; 44:8; 45:5, 6, 14, 21f.; 46:9) and draws a remarkably strong contrast between the one true God and the gods of the heathen.

In fact, our prophet stresses the nothingness of these
false gods in comparison with Israel's God. The power-
lessness of these false gods is keenly accentuated in the
light of Yahweh's limitless power. For Yahweh controls
the stars of the heavens, and even calls them all by name
(41:26). Moreover, He conditions the stream of history
by initiating the world-revolution which sees Cyrus as
the chief instrument of God's redemptive purpose. The
idols and their devotees, however, find themselves com-
pletely helpless before Him (cf. 41:1ff.; 41:21ff.; 43:
9ff.; 44:6ff.).

The monotheism which is reflected so clearly here in
Second Isaiah did not develop from mere philosophical
speculation. It emerged, as Walther Eichrodt reminds
us, out of Israel's "experience of God's close and living
reality. . . . It was only because their God Yahweh was
at hand to dominate the whole of life and to give practical proof of his reality that Israel's picture of God was
able to grow. . . ."[3]

*b. God's Holiness*

For Second Isaiah, holiness is the singular or unique
attribute of God (40:25b). The Hebrew word for holiness (*qadhosh*) occurs eleven times in the block of chapters assigned to this prophet (41:14, 16, 20; 43:3, 14;
47:4; 48:17; 49:7 (twice); 54:5; 55:5). In the prophecy
of Isaiah "the holiness of God stands over against all that
is human, in contrast to everything worldly. . . . But in
Second Isaiah the conception is combined with others,
most notably with Redeemer: 'Your Redeemer is the
Holy One of Israel' (41:14); . . .(cf. 54:5; 43:3, 14; 47:

4; 49:7). . . . . Yahweh's holiness, while uniquely and peculiarly his, manifests itself in mighty acts and wonders, but supremely in the redemption of his people. . . ."4

In Second Isaiah holiness is intimately related to the royal majesty of Yahweh. It means "him who is unapproachable because of his complete 'otherness' and perfection when compared with all created things."5

## 2. *His Activity*

The creative activity of God is undoubtedly the strong point in our prophet's thought. But this is not strange. It emerged as a logical consequence of the historical situation. The Israelites were filled with despair and burdened with despondency (cf. 40:27). Their questions and doubts concerning God's sovereignty prompted the prophet to portray in detail the manner in which their God had created the seas, the heaven, and the earth—the whole cosmos. Indeed, argues the prophet, history is sustained by this same creative God; therefore, there should not be the slightest doubt as to the achievement of His ultimate purpose.6

The purpose of God's creative activity is clearly delineated by Second Isaiah. He creates in order that He may redeem. In emphasizing the creative activity of God, the prophet employs a number of verbs, but the ones most often used are *Yaṣar* and *Bara*. This latter verb, for instance, appears at least sixteen times (40: 26, 28; 41:20; 42:5; 43:1, 7, 15; 45:7 (twice), 8, 12, 18 (twice); 48:7; 54:16 (twice). As this verb is used by our prophet it obviously refers "to a unique creative action

which he alone can perform."[7]    Thus, revelatory insights emerge from His creative activity. Not only is His
might revealed; His wisdom and unaided initiative are
disclosed (40:13-14).  In the words of a contemporary
theologian, "the character of the divine life is made
manifest in revelation."[8]

But the most important thing which can be said about
His creative activity is that it does not stand alone. His
creation is for redemptive purposes.  The world was
made to be inhabited (45:12, 18); and those whom He
created in His own image were made to be saved. This,
obviously, is His purpose throughout the whole of the
prophecy. Thus, it may be said that "creation is the initial act of which redemption is the finale."[9]

### a.  God's Righteousness

Closely coupled with God's creative activity is the
concept of God's righteousness.  The Old Testament
usage of the word righteousness, it should be explained,
points up the idea of right behavior or a right disposition, and is descriptive of both human beings and
God.  In the Old Testament usage, the norm of one's
disposition or behavior is discovered in the terms of
the covenant.[10]

For Second Isaiah, God's righteousness becomes most
clear in His work of salvation.  His redemptive acts
which were calculated to bring His erring people back
into a covenantal relationship were all expressions of His
righteousness, as well as expressions of His covenant
love, loyalty, and kindness (42:6, 21; 45:8, 13; 46:13;
51:6).

## b.  God's Love

God's love, of course, cannot be dissociated from His creative activity and from the expressions of His righteousness.  For it was His love which gave substance and meaning to all of these expressions.  In fact, it may be said that the prophetic understanding of God's love finds new dimensions in the thought of this prophet.

Second Isaiah seems to have found new terms in which to proclaim God's inexhaustibly-rich love.  "Israel, the divorced wife, now degraded to the position of a slave, a dishonoured captive, a childless widow loaded with ignominy, would be brought out of her misery and showered with abundant blessing as a bride beloved, a joyful mother of many children, a princess re-instated in her position of honour (40:2; 49:14ff., 20ff.; 50:1; 51:17ff.; 54:1f., 6f.; 60:4ff., 15; 62:4)."[11]  Although other prophets had spoken tenderly of God's love, no one spoke with greater tenderness nor with greater imagination than did the prophet of the Exile (cf. esp. 49:15).

With all of his accent on God's love for Israel, there is no indication that Second Isaiah was not fully aware of the nation's guilt.  Scattered throughout his work are certain reproaches (42:18-25; 43:22-27; 45:9-13; 48:1-11; 50:1f.) which tend to magnify the remission vouchsafed to the recalcitrant people.  Hence, the prophet appeals to those who are bogged down so obstinately in utter despair to accept God's offer of love.  For after all, as he reasons, there is no *legal* obstacle to Yahweh's taking Israel back.  No bill of divorcement was ever executed (50:1ff.).  With such accent on the marriage-bond between Yahweh and Israel, the prophet quite naturally thinks of God as the *go'el,* the Redeemer, who is obligated to rescue His near of kin (43:3; 49:26), who now has received a double amount of punishment for her sins (40:2; 54:6ff.).

In summary, Second Isaiah shared the view of other prophets—namely, that God was known in the concrete relation of fellowship. God takes the initiative and reveals Himself. Thus, it is in the covenant of God with Israel that there is to be found "the point of intersection of all the major lines of the knowledge of God. . ., just as in the New Testament this point of intersection lies in the Word's becoming flesh, . . ."[12]

The manner in which He revealed Himself will now engage our attention as we turn to Second Isaiah's concept of the covenant.

## II. The Covenant

The Biblical category which provides the controlling unity of the Scriptures and which dramatizes the persistent activity of God among His people is that of the covenant. Since that is true, and since the Second Isaiah's thought must be viewed against the general concept of covenant, it will be instructive to set forth some general observations on the covenant idea before proceeding to the specific consideration of Second Isaiah's views. These observations, to be the most meaningful to the reader, must embrace a definition of covenant, the history and types of covenantal relationships, the theological presuppositions which undergird this concept, and the influence of the covenant idea upon God's people.

*I.*

The Hebrew word for covenant is *berith.* The ety-
mology of this word in Hebrew is not very clear. It may
be derived from the Akkadian *baru,* "to bind," or "to
fetter." A number of the Biblical references to *berith*
suggest rather pointedly this sense of a binding together
—this bond which unites the people to God.[13] Again, it
is quite possible that the noun *berith* is derived from the
verb *barah,* which means "to eat."[14] This meaning
would suit some of the contexts quite well, and would
give proper emphasis to the cultic meal which accom-
panied the making of the covenant (cf. Exodus 24:
5-11).

This latter meaning is buttressed by the fact that the
verb *karath* ("to cut") is often coupled with the noun
*berith.* In other words, the Hebrews spoke not of "making a covenant" but of "cutting a covenant" *(karath
berith).*[15] In some instances, the two parties to the
covenant would cut an animal in two with the two halves
representing the parties to the covenant. The blood of
the slain animal would then in some mystical way effect
a unity of the two parties to the covenant, since it was
believed that the blood represented the seat of life (cf.
Lev. 17:11; Jer. 34:18).[16]

It would appear that both of these meanings may have
been embraced in the Hebraic concept of covenant—the
covenant made at Sinai which described Israel's unique
relationship with God. It is true that the word covenant was used to describe other special relationships
which existed between human beings on the horizontal
plane—between man and man or between nation and

nation (I Samuel 18:3; 20:16; Exodus 23:32). But the covenant *par excellence,* the covenant made at Sinai, was infused with the greatest possible meaning for Israel. It spoke eloquently of God's mighty act of redemption, His reaching down into the life of an insignificant people and delivering them from bondage and then calling them unto Himself for a special vocation (Exodus 19: 4, 5, 6).

The corollary of this call was Israel's response, which emerged (it should be noticed) in an atmosphere of trust, confidence, and security. From the earliest times Israel had experienced not only the power but the goodness and faithfulness of God. Thus, she willingly submitted to the will of the Deity as this will was expressed in the Decalogue and in the Book of the Covenant. This divine will established not only the moral and social way of living but, even more, the means for holding the tribes together and maintaining a distinctive redemptive community. Indeed, in the relationship established by the covenant Israel clearly confesses that God is her sovereign Lord and she is His people (Exodus 19:6; I Samuel 8:4-9).

The terms employed to describe this unique covenantal relationship are quite meaningful. Israel is not normally labeled *goi* (or nation) in the Old Testament. She is more often known as the *'am yahweh* (the people of Yahweh). The *'am yahweh* is also the *qahal* (the people who hear His voice—*qol*), and are thus "called out" from among other peoples and nations. The *qahal* is thus formed because He has chosen (*bahar*) Israel as a peculiar possession (*segullah*—Exodus 19:5), and because

Israel has responded to His call. Thus, Israel, the covenant people, becomes the *'edah* or the "congregation" of
the faithful whose responsibility it is to fulfill not only
His will but His purpose within their lives. The *'am yahweh,* the *qahal,* the *'edah,* the *'am qadhosh* (holy people),
of the Old Testament may thus be equated with the
*ecclesia* of the New Testament. Accordingly, the entity
formed as a result of the covenant was a religious and
not a political community[17]—hence the strong emphasis
which we find upon keeping the covenantal community
free and distinct from the surrounding cultural influ-
ences (Lev. 19:2; *et. al.*).

The sense of community which developed out of this
concept of covenant was unusually strong in Israel.
True, the individual was important, but his importance
was discovered as he related himself to the larger group.
Here he could be delivered from his self-centeredness
or self-idolatry, and thus find his true life in "a calling
within the community." In this calling his own election
"is understood to fulfill a portion of the community
election, when, in complete loyalty to the Lord, who
binds all diversity into unity, he discovers the time of
his life to be overarched by the time of the new community, which in turn is transcended by the redemptive
purpose of God."[18]   In obedient service, in true parti-
cipation within the covenantal community, the individual fulfills his God-given vocation.

This sense of covenant did not stop here. It actually
bound all of the Israelites into one organic whole.
Accordingly, they felt that the covenantal relationship
involved a "psychic union of souls," a mutuality or in-

termingling of life." Thus, no one could find meaning or purpose for his life outside this relationship. Indeed, to be deprived of the community's privileges, protection, and blessings constituted one of the worst punishments or tragedies of life (cf. Cain, Gen. 4:10-14).[19]

2.

It should be said at this point that this idea of covenant which expressed so poignantly the special relationship which existed between Israel and God was not an indigenous idea. Moreover, the covenant concept was not derived from religious but from legal practices. The archaeological evidence indicates that covenants were effected far back in ancient times, long before the days of Moses. There are references to international covenants in old Sumerian texts of the third millennium B.C., "and it would seem likely that covenants upheld by oath must go back many centuries if not millennia before."[20] We have, however, a very limited amount of source material for studying international covenants, possibly because of "the accidents of transmission or excavation." The material available to us comes from the Hittite Empire, from the period 1450-1200 B.C. Although the material is limited, it is extremely valuable because it comes from a time contemporary with the emergence of the people of Israel.[21]

The Hittites borrowed the covenant form from the East, since the form was common property in the secular world of the second millennium B.C. The types of covenant illustrated in the Hittite documents were of two major kinds: (1) Suzerainty; and (2) Parity. The basic difference between the two is this: in the former, only the inferior is bound by an oath; but in the latter, both parties are bound to obey identical stipulations. The suzerainty treaty, however, is the basic kind and is most illuminating in our attempt to understand the Biblical idea of covenant.

The suzerainty treaty among the Hittites was the means whereby a king bound his vassals to himself in a relationship of faithfulness and obedience. The primary purpose of this relationship was to foster the interests of the Hittite sovereign. Thus, it was really unilateral in nature, for the stipulations of the treaty were binding upon the vassal alone. Only the vassal assumed the oath of obedience, since it was reasoned that if the sovereign took obligations upon himself this would constitute an abridgement of his sovereignty and his exclusive right of self-determination.[22] But even though this was urged, it was still emphasized that the vassal should trust the benevolence of his Lord.

The student of the Bible detects some points of contact between the Hittite suzerainty treaty and the covenant which God made (or cut) with Israel. An analysis of the elements which go to make up the Hititte treaty will make this even more apparent. The six principal elements are as follows:

*1—Preamble.* This introductory element identifies the author of the treaty or covenant, and sets forth his titles and attributes as well as his genealogy. The dominant emphasis in this section is upon the majesty and power of the king who confers this covenantal relationship upon his vassal.

*2—The historical prologue.* This section of the treaty outlines the previous relations which have existed between the two parties. Much is made here of the benevolent deeds which the Hittite sovereign has already done for his vassal.[23] These deeds are not stereotyped, however, but are careful descriptions of actual events. Thus, the vassal is impressed with the fact that his gratitude to the great and benevolent king should be perpetual because of what he has already received!

*3—The stipulations.* The obligations imposed upon the vassal are stated in this section. The vassal is ordinarily prohibited from establishing any relationships outside the Hittite Empire. Moreover, he cannot offer any resistance to the sovereignty of the Hittite king. Accordingly, he cannot become the slave or dependent of any other person. In the event of war, he must provide support for the Hittite king or for anyone else whose primary subservience is to the great king. "The vassal must appear before the Hittite king once a year, probably on the occasion of annual tribute (cf. Ex. 23:17)."[24]

*4—Provision for deposit in the temple and periodic public reading.* The treaty was sacred in that the deity offered the necessary protection to insure that it was kept intact. Moreover, since it involved not only the vassal king but his entire constituency, periodic public reading familiarized the populace with their obligations to the great king, and reminded them anew of the warm relationship which their king had with the "mighty and majestic Emperor."

*5—The list of gods as witnesses.* Just as there were witnesses to a legal contract, so the gods were construed as not only witnesses to the international covenants but the actual enforcers as well (cf. Ezekiel 17:12-21).

6—*The curses and blessings formula.* The curses and blessings which are outlined in the texts constitute the actions of the gods (cf. Deut. 28). The Hittite king, in the event of a breach in the covenant, would initiate military reprisals, possibly as the agent of the deity (?).[25]

The covenant forms in Israel reflect rather clearly some of these elements which have just been set forth. But, more importantly, some of these elements help to underscore a signal feature of the Biblical idea of covenant—namely, the suzerainty or sovereignty of God, the fact that God and man are not on the same plane. In the *berith,* God remained God; He remained supreme; He remained on the higher level.

To correct a rather common misunderstanding, it should be emphatically stressed that the covenant relationship was freely assumed on God's part; "it was no compulsory bond of God with his people. God existed before the nation; and he was independent of his people. God could dissolve the relationship any time he pleased. . . ."[26] Certainly Yahweh was not legally bound to Israel. In no sense could it be said that His sovereignty was limited by the covenant.[27] Since the covenant was freely initiated—*initiated as a gift of grace*—God was perfectly free to terminate it at His pleasure. But, as the prophets witness quite poignantly, God's love constrains Him to remain faithful to the covenant (cf. Hosea 11: 1-9; Ezekiel 16:1-63) because the covenant He makes is an everlasting covenant (*berith ῾olam*—Isaiah 54:8; 55:3).

*3.*

The theological bases or presuppositions of the covenant are indicated clearly in the Scriptures. They center chiefly around the doctrines of revelation and election.

The establishment of the covenantal relationship through the work of Moses emphasizes the *reality* of the divine revelation. God is not some nebulous or abstract idea. Neither is His self-disclosure something that must be grasped speculatively. From the standpoint of the Old Testament, God breaks in on the life of His people and demonstrates His presence and love for them through His mighty acts which are calculated to be redemptive in nature (cf. Ps. 103:7; *et. al.*).[28] Actually, just as it has been so well observed, "the Old Testament is the narration of God's action: what he has done, is doing, and will do. All human history is the theatre of his self-disclosure, and nature too is his handiwork. . . ."[29] God, then, was very real and personal to Israel!

The Scriptures indicate, however, that the purpose and content of revelation are practical and not doctrinal. In other words, the object of God's self-disclosure is not the satisfaction of man's insatiable curiosity but "guidance in the way of life" (Deut. 29:29; 30:15-20; John 10:10; 20:31; II Timothy 3:16).[30] The corollary of this revelation of His will and way of salvation might very well be the revelation of much of His nature, but the latter is manifestly of lesser importance and concern than the former.

The second doctrine or basis of the covenant is that of election. It is this doctrine which makes possible the whole concept of covenant. Therefore, regardless of one's own prejudices or point of view, he must take this doctrine seriously if he is to understand the theology of the Old Testament. For this idea is manifestly the primary article of Israel's faith.

The doctrine of election is centered in the fact of the Exodus, the crucial or pivotal event in the history of Israel. In fact, it was this event which made her a self-conscious historical community. In expressing the content of her faith, Israel joyfully proclaimed that God had heard the cry of an oppressed people in Egyptian bondage and through His mighty acts had caused them to be delivered. After this signal deliverance, He called or elected the people for a special purpose (cf. Ex. 19:5; Deut. 7:6).

This apparent particularism in the operation of divine grace has subjected the Biblical faith to much criticism. Therefore, it should be observed, just as the Scriptures attest (cf. Isaiah 40-55), that Israel's election "was not for selfish or self-centered privilege. . . ."[31] Israel was chosen for a special purpose—namely, to make Him known among the peoples and nations and in general to foster His purpose of redemption among men (Isaiah 42: 6ff.; 49:1-7; Ex. 19:6).

H. H. Rowley has observed that the problems incident to election may be readily resolved when the subject is viewed teleologically. In other words, election is for a purpose. Therefore, God chooses those who are the most suited to fulfill His purpose. Favoritism or discrimination does not enter into the choice, for God has not withheld His revelation from man anywhere. The determining factor has been man himself—his capacity

and willingness to receive God's revelation and to enter
into a dynamic and intimate relationship with his
sovereign Lord.[32]

*4.*

The relationship effected through the call or election
of Israel is a unique one, and is given form and special
meaning in terms of the covenant. The covenant bound
God's people to Him in a solemn and sacred "relationship of obligation and obedience." The ratification of
the covenant was achieved through a very moving and
meaningful rite—a rite which mystically joined God and
people together in a sacred union (Ex. 24:6-8; cf. also
Gal. 2:20).[33]   However, just as it has been previously
indicated, this union was not of equals. It was a relationship of servants to a ruler. God was accepted as King,
as Sovereign, as Lord. As their King, He would provide
justice for them, as well as salvation and security. The
people, in turn, were to hearken unto Him, to serve
Him, and to be obedient to His will.

The constitution of the covenant society was embraced within the law which God gave. Contrary to
what has been popularly held, the law (when rightly
conceived) was not "a penal burden to be borne" but a
*means of grace!* The law, within the covenantal framework, was an expression of God's will. To keep it, then,
meant life, and health, and peace. Through this law the
total community (or, for that matter, each individual
within the community) could find justice and security.

George Ernest Wright has reminded us that Israel's
law was not a natural law. It was God's special gift to

His covenant people. Accordingly, the law was "rooted in the grace of God and conceived as a special revelation."[34] Thus, for God's people "totalitarian rule was lifted from the earthly to the cosmic sphere"—from the human king to the divine King. To keep this relationship intact God's people were required faithfully to fulfill His will on both the vertical and horizontal levels. For anything which tended to disrupt community was construed not only as sin but as a breakdown of this primal relationship which gave meaning, purpose and direction to life. It was, therefore, incumbent upon every responsible individual to keep *chesed,* to remain steadfast in his love and devotion to God, and to maintain a relationship of righteousness and justice toward his fellowman. In an attempt to maintain this kind of community, the prophets of Israel constantly summoned their people to renew their covenantal relationship with God, in the profound realization that their specific sins were merely symptomatic of this broken relationship (cf. Jeremiah 2:13; Hosea 6:6). To keep the covenant intact, the prophets taught, it was incumbent upon every individual "to do justly, and to love mercy, and to walk humbly with. . .God" (Micah 6:8).

The prophetic interpretation of the covenant comes to fruition in the thought of Second Isaiah. Like the earlier prophets, he has nothing to say about the covenant at Sinai. He does, of course, deal with the deliverance from Egypt and is obviously aware that Yahweh chose this people for Himself (43:16f.; 51:9f.; 52:4; 44:21, 24). But in thinking of the ideal conditions which will exist ultimately, when God's redemptive purpose for Israel and the world is realized, Second Isaiah describes this in terms of a *berith* (covenant) (Isa. 54:10; 55:3). He links this with the past, however, through the election of Abraham (Isa. 41:8f.; 51:2) and his emphasis upon God's faithfulness which causes His former work to come to completion (Isa. 42:6, 21; 46:3f.). For Second Isaiah the divine activity was constant; thus faith was not to be kindled *solely* from any prior act or historical institution, such as the Sinai covenant, important as it manifestly was in the life and history of Israel.

The prophet of the Exile now has his thought centered on a new and most decisive event. In fact, all former blessings would now be dwarfed by the "new thing" which Yahweh was about to do—by "the unheard-of revelation of salvation now standing at their very doors" (43:18f.; 54:4).[35]  Indeed, the old covenant is to be overshadowed by the eternal covenant of peace—a covenant that will bring welfare, harmony, and total prosperity.

The new covenant which Yahweh is to confer upon Israel will bring favor like that which He showed to David. According to Isaiah 55:4, David was a witness, a leader, and a commander to the people. Similarly, Israel will one day gather about her unknown nations which have recognized the power of Yahweh and which desire to know more about Him (Isaiah 55:5).[36]

God's righteousness or faithfulness where his covenant is concerned is particularly stressed by the prophets. Thus, it is not unusual that Second Isaiah speaks repeatedly of Yahweh's *ṣedakah* (faithfulness). In fact, he makes use of this to encourage the exiles. For both the prophet and the people this became the guarantee of the re-establishment of the people. In Second Isaiah there is really no difference between Yahweh's righteousness and His mercy or favor. Thus, *sedakah* is practically equivalent to salvation or deliverance, just as is seen in Isaiah 46:13: "I bring near my deliverance (*sedakah*), it is not far off, and my salvation will not tarry."

The above discussion of the covenant indicates something of the importance of this concept in the life and history of Israel, particularly as it conditioned their thoughts about other facets of their religion. We shall notice this particularly in the following treatment.

### III. Sin

Sin, of course, must be viewed from the standpoint of the covenant, because it is the covenant which not only conditions all relationships but actually upholds all life.[37]    Through the covenant "the totalities and organisms are formed in which life acts." Righteousness, therefore, results from the maintenance of the covenant. On the other hand, however, sin or unrighteousness consists in violating the laws of the covenant— acting outside its prescriptions and proscriptions for human life.

It is thus sin to hate one's brother (Lev. 19:17), or to act indifferently toward him (Genesis 42:22; 50:17). Indeed, whenever we examine any of the human actions which are characterized by the name of sin, we find that the underlying cause is a breach of the covenant. Consequently, when one does not give his neighbor what the law entitles him to, one commits a sin against him. This very fact suggests clearly that sin is determined by the relationship which exists among men.

As we have tried to explain previously, the covenantal community was regarded as an intermingling of lives or souls. In such a psychic community, anything which tended to disrupt this mystical relationship was construed as sinful.

Johannes Pedersen explains that the covenant idea was so all-inclusive that it even conditioned one's relationship to the earth. Thus, one must deal kindly with it and not exploit it, for the latter would be construed as sin.[38]

According to Israelite thought, the Law was the most significant part of God's revelation, because it set forth His will for mankind. In a sense, it was the Divine constitution for the regulation of society. Man's primary duty, therefore, is to obey this Law. If he does not, then he is guilty of sin; he has rebelled against God.[39]

Since it is God who enters into the covenantal relationship with man, sin is anything which tends to impair or to break this relationship. Indeed, the whole sin vocabulary supports this fundamental idea of "breaking." *Ḥata'* is the missing, the abandoning of the straight road. *'Awon* is to turn aside or to become lost, not only in act but also in thought. *Ma'al* is unfaithfulness, while *pesha'* is open rebellion. Thus, wherever any of the preceding expresses itself it breaks down the divine-human relationship and man is guilty of sin.

The Old Testament generally speaks of man as a sinner, not because he is a human being but because he has consistently rebelled against his God and followed his own bent. Man has failed to understand that in the covenant relationship God is Sovereign Lord and he is His servant, and that it is incumbent upon him to obey His law and to fulfill His sovereign purpose.[40]

Second Isaiah, just like the other prophets, believed that sin is a violation of God's law. In fact, this prophet held that the exile itself was punishment which Yahweh imposed upon His people because of their sins (42:24f.; 43:27f.; 47:6; 50:1f.). But, in Second Isaiah's thought, the sin has now been doubly paid for (40:2). Unlike some of the other prophets, however, who place emphasis upon personal repentance (cf. Amos 5:6f.; Hosea 14:1ff.), Second Isaiah contends that it is Yahweh Himself who blots out Israel's sins and restores her to her homeland. In fact, during the exile the people made no effort to win His favor by offerings presented to Him (43:22-44:5). But this is of no apparent moment. For the sake of His name and for the vindication of His honor, Yahweh mercifully effects this restoration (48: 9, 11; 52:5f.) for His people—a people who now bear His law in their hearts.[41]

The grace of God thus transcends whatever judgment may be deserved. The prophet at this point plays well the role of pastor. It may have been that this oracle of forgiveness was addressed to the people on a day of repentance.[42] But the central religious truth that is so strongly pointed up, regardless of whatever else may be implied in this passage, is that "forgiveness is a permanent condition in the heart of God." This is a part of God's nature, an expression of His sovereign love for His covenant-people.[43] The motive for the forgiveness, of course, is the covenant bond.

Above everything else, it must be remembered that our prophet is thinking in eschatological terms, just as it will be explained in our subsequent treatment. Eschatological time, therefore, "is the time of forgiveness."[44] Thus, the theological problems which may arise in one's mind as he contemplates the divine mercy may then be resolved. For a new time is beginning! The grace, love, power, and salvation of God are now to be experienced in a deeper dimension. The full meaning of covenant is also now to be revealed in the "new thing"—the eschatological fulfillment (48:3-8), which we shall describe in detail in the following pages.

In the meantime, however, we must define the meaning of prophetic eschatology. This we shall do in the following chapter.

## NOTES AND REFERENCES

1. Walther Eichrodt, *Theology of The Old Testament,* trans. J. A. Baker (Philadelphia: The Westminster Press, 1960), I, 33, 286.

2. *Ibid.,* pp. 178ff.

3. *Ibid.,* p. 227.

4. James Muilenburg, "Isaiah 40-66," *The Interpreter's Bible* (New York: Abingdon Press, 1956), V, 400.

5. Eichrodt, *op. cit.,* p. 273.

6. Muilenburg, *op. cit.,* p. 435.

7. *Ibid.,* p. 401.

8. Paul Tillich, *Systematic Theology* (Chicago: The University of Chicago Press, 1951), I, 243.

9. Muilenburg, *op. cit.,* p. 402; G. Von Rad, *Old Testament*

*Theology* (New York: Harper & Row, Publishers, 1965), II, 240.

10. Eichrodt, *op. cit.*, p. 240.

11. *Ibid.*, p. 255.

12. *Ibid.*, p. 518.

13. Henry S. Gehman, "The Covenant—The Old Testament Foundation of the Church," *Theology Today*, VII (April 1950-January 1951), pp. 26ff.

14. James Muilenburg, *The Way of Israel* (New York: Harper & Brothers Publishers, 1961), p. 55.

15. Cf. Genesis 15:10; Exodus 24:8; *et al.*

16. W. O. E. Oesterley, *Hebrew Religion: Its Origin and Development* (New York: The Macmillan Company, 1930), pp. 139-140.

17. George A. F. Knight, *A Christian Theology of The Old Testament* (Richmond: John Knox Press, 1959), pp. 223, 224; Gehman, *op. cit.*, p. 28; John Bright, *The Kingdom of God* (New York: Abingdon Press, 1953), *passim.*

18. George Ernest Wright, *The Rule of God* (Garden City: Doubleday & Company, Inc., 1960), p. 45.

19. Wright, "The Faith of Israel," *The Interpreter's Bible* (Nashville: Abingdon Press, 1952), I, 354.

20. George E. Mendenhall, "Covenant Forms in Israelite Traditions," *The British Archaeologist*, XVII (September 1954), p. 53.

21. *Ibid.*

22. *Ibid.*, p. 56.

23. Notice this emphasis especially in Israel's little liturgy or confession of faith (Deut. 26:5-10), as well as in the historical prologue to the Ten Commandments (Ex. 20:2). Law, it should be noted, is preceded by gospel!

24. Mendenhall, *op. cit.*, p. 59.

25. *Ibid.*, p. 60.

26. Gehman, *op. cit.*, p. 30.

27.   Bernhard W. Anderson, *Understanding The Old Testament* (Englewood Cliffs: Prentice Hall, Inc., 1957), p. 57.

28.   Eichrodt, *op. cit.,* p. 37.

29.   Anderson, *op. cit.,* p. 5.

30.   Millar Burrows, *An Outline of Biblical Theology* (Philadelphia: The Westminster Press, 1946), pp. 12-13.

31.   Wright, "The Faith of Israel," *op. cit.,* p. 354.

32.   H. H. Rowley, *The Biblical Doctrine of Election* (London: Lutterworth Press, 1948), p. 39.

33.   Hosea's introduction of the marriage metaphor offered an unusually effective way of describing the covenantal relationship between God and Israel.

34.   "The Faith of Israel," *op. cit.,* pp. 355, 356.

35.   Eichrodt, *op. cit.,* p. 62.

36.   Johannes Lindblom, *Prophecy In Ancient Israel* (Philadelphia: Muhlenburg Press, 1962), p. 382.

37.   Johs. Pedersen, *Israel: Its Life and Culture* (London: Oxford University Press, 1926), I-II, 414-415.

38.   *Ibid.,* p. 479.

39.   George Ernest Wright, *The Challenge of Israel's Faith* (Chicago: The University of Chicago Press, 1943), p. 42.

40.   Edmund Jacob, *Theology Of The Old Testament* (New York: Harper & Brothers Publishers, 1958), pp. 281-284.

41.   Pedersen, *op. cit.,* pp. 600-601.

42.   Muilenburg, "Isaiah 40-66," *op. cit.,* p. 497.

43.   *Ibid.,* p. 498.

44.   *Ibid.,* p. 500.

## Chapter 4

## PROPHETIC ESCHATOLOGY

### I. *Definition*

Eschatology has been defined traditionally as "the doctrine of the last things" or "the doctrine concerning the last things. . . ."[1] Some writers consider the following to be essential elements in this definition: man's condition after death, the destiny of the nations, the end of the world, the Messiah, the kingdom of heaven on earth, the intermediate state, the resurrection, the destruction of the world, the new heaven and the new earth.[2] It is apparent, of course, that there is some overlapping in the listing of these elements, but the list includes both the earlier and the later elements in Jewish thought.

Hugo Gressmann, on the other hand, narrows this definition considerably. He holds that eschatology is limited to a consideration of the end of the world and its renovation. Thus, there is excluded in his thinking those things pertaining to death and resurrection for the individual.[3]

It is the present writer's opinion that Gressmann's more limited definition may be correct where the earlier Israelite conception of eschatology is concerned, but it is hardly adequate to describe the burgeoning and flowering concepts subsequent to the Exile. This thought is

91

well stated by Schmidt when he says: ". . .Eschatology clearly develops with the growth of man's intellectual and moral perceptions, his larger social experience, and his expanding knowledge of nature."[4]

T. C. Vriezen explains that the term "eschatology" may have deeper signification when it is defined in the light of Hebraic understanding. He maintains that when the word is employed in its wider sense it can denote the *faith* that "knows of a *new Kingdom,* a new world, even if there is no question here of the destruction of the cosmos and even if we see that it is all enacted within the framework of this one world of God." But most importantly, it is instructive for one to remember that Hebrew thought has only one word (*'aharit*) to designate *future* and *end, later* and *last.*[5]

More explicitly, Vriezen shows how the Hebraic concept of time is markedly different from the ordinary idea. Unlike the Western practice of dividing time into separate periods with, perhaps, separate names, Hebrew thought has no idea of time and, consequently, cannot divide it. This way of thinking, then, is characterized as "totalizing" and not "analytical."[6] In relating this idea to eschatology, Vriezen explains that the term can be used to refer to a renewal that falls within the bounds of history, simply because "Hebrew thought does not make such a sharp distinction between the historical and the supra-historical as we do."[7]

Amos Wilder sees a close relationship between eschatology and myth. In fact, he feels that the former can best be understood from the analogy of myth, because myth deals symbolically with the "unknown origins and the unknown past." Accordingly, eschatology may be defined as "that form of myth which accounts for the unknown future."[8]

Since the word "myth" has been not only an opprobrious term in some circles, but a vague one also, it is perhaps well to remind the reader that the great myths of history and religion have been "summary representations of essential truths." That is to say, myths have objectivized in a singular way the nature and soul of the particular people or race.[9]

In terms of myth, then, Jewish eschatology conveys great spiritual truths, just as great art does likewise. Behind the eschatology was the inspiring force of intuition with reference to the future. The resulting scheme might, of course, give an imperfect forecast of world history, but like the best myth it symbolized the essential intuition. Eschatologies naturally vary in keeping with the religious intuitions out of which they are constructed.

The writer's own definition of eschatology embraces elements from both Vriezen and Wilder. In other words, he accepts the broad definition of prophetic eschatology, which conceived of a new kingdom enacted within this present cosmos. As Carl Steuernagel has reminded, the structural lines of Jewish eschatology are not always too sharply defined. This is true, but it is obvious that in the older prophets the eschatology must be described more in nationalistic terms, while in the later or apocalyptic works the eschatology moves outside the frame of this world, and must be described in universal or transcendent terms.[10]

The prophets, especially Second Isaiah, reveal clearly their foreshortened perspectives. This may well be attributed to the keenness and immediacy of the prophets' perception of the inevitable triumph of God's purpose. At any rate, in describing this coming new age they were compelled to use the only available tool for such expression—the myth. This tool, it must be remembered, had been employed to describe the beginning and, by the same kind of reasoning, had to be employed to describe the closing events.

## II.   Origin and History

There seem to be at least two schools of thought with reference to the origin of Hebrew eschatology. One school holds that the eschatological antecedents must be sought in antiquity. The other school holds that Hebrew eschatology had a comparatively late development.

Hugo Gressmann has been one of the principal exponents of the first-mentioned view. According to his theory, many myths of foreign origin infiltrated into the Israelite culture long before the time of Amos. These myths, in turn, influenced the people's thinking about Yahweh, His relationship with His people and with the nations of the world. The most important concept among these myths was that of the coming destruction of the earth by fire. Preceding this destruction was to be a series of plagues. But following the destruction of the world there would be a renewal and a return of the primeval paradise, with its innocence and bliss. This earthly paradise would be ruled by the first man, who would assume a semi-divine form. It has been conjectured that this idea arose in Persia, and then came by way of Elam to Babylonia, possibly as early as 2000 B.C. Later on the Amorites were responsible for bringing it to Palestine where, by the eighth century B.C., it had become saturated with the Israelite spirit.[11]

It appears that the great prophets modified this myth somewhat, except where they made "concessions to the popular eschatology." These prophets obviously applied the myth relating to the cosmic catastrophe to a much more limited area, perhaps to their own land or to that small segment of the earth with which they were familiar. What is more, because of their strong moral convictions they were inclined to suppress the element of hope in the myth—that which spoke in terms of the cosmic restoration.[12]

Other writers agree with Gressmann. For example, Oesterley and Robinson contend that the eschatological thought among the Hebrews dates from an early period.[13] They cite as evidence the ancient but popular idea of the "Day of Yahweh." The way in which Amos deals with this popular concept reveals that the people had long been familiar with the event that would ostensibly bring judgment upon all their enemies and peace and prosperity to themselves. Indeed, say these critics, "there is much in the prophetical books and elsewhere which makes it clear that the circle of ideas connected with the eschatological outlook goes back to far more ancient times. . . ."[14]

Some of the more recent writers share the same opinion. John Bright, for instance, claims that Israel's faith "was strongly eschatological in orientation." This developed from their strong belief that history was moving to a God-directed destination.

Bright does admit, however, that it might not be proper to use the term "eschatology" in reference to this early faith of Israel. But he does believe that the germs of it were present in this faith. Indeed, he feels that an embryonic "eschatology" may even be detected in ancient epics of the patriarchs.[15]

On the other hand, there are those critics who maintain that Hebrew eschatology had its origin in the exilic or post-exilic period. Chief among these has been Julius Wellhausen. Those scholars in the Wellhausen school argue that the bulk of the eschatological passages in the pre-exilic prophets represent post-exilic interpolations.[16]

Sigmund Mowinckel holds that Hebrew eschatology arose after the fall of the Southern Kingdom. Upon developing, this eschatology reproduced the salient features of the New Year ritual and its related mythology: (1) Kingship of Yahweh; (2) catastrophes in nature; (3) deliverance from enemies as a result of the divine conflict with hostile powers; (4) judgment; (5) the remnant; (6) the new creation; (7) the new covenant; (8) the eschatological banquet (the sacrificial meal); (9) and the Messiah, the divinely appointed ruler.[17]

It is evident from the foregoing that, according to Mowinckel's view, eschatology was nothing more than a futuristic projection of the dramatic cultic ritual. The divine power which was currently experienced, and which was renewed in the annual festival, was transformed into a future hope. The Day of Yahweh, the central element in the eschatological drama, was merely derived "from the day of Yahweh's enthronement in the festival. It has become the future, final, and decisive day, when, once for all, Yahweh was to assert His kingship."[18]

Julian Morgenstern has more recently contended that the "proximate origin" of the above-mentioned concept was the observance of the New Year's Day in the fall. His approach is somewhat different from Mowinckel's, however, as the following discussion will show.

It is to be noted that although Morgenstern's "proximate origin" for the Day of Yahweh is *comparatively* late, it is still considerably earlier than Mowinckel's date. Morgenstern believes the concept developed from the ritual that was conducted in Solomon's Temple in Jerusalem. On New Year's Day, when the rising sun sent its rays through the eastern gate into the *debir* at the opposite end of the sanctuary, it was believed that Yahweh had entered into the Temple and had taken His place upon the throne as the divine King, there to fix the fortune and destiny of His people for the ensuing year.

Although tracing the more recent origin of the Day of Yahweh from the tenth century B.C., Morgenstern detects the roots of this concept in antiquity. He says:

> But in its ultimate origins the concept reached back far beyond this to Phoenician and North Semitic, and even to general mythological and religious concept, belief, and practice of early Semitic agricultural peoples, to the great struggle at the very beginning of existence, the first New Year's Day, the struggle and victory of light over darkness. of good over evil, or Marduk over Tiamat, of 'Al'eyan Ba'al over Mot, of life over death, of resurrection and renewed

life over eternal negation of existence in the dark and deep
nether-world. The basic idea was general among agricultural
Semitic peoples. It came to Israel definitely. . . in the time
of Solomon through Phoenician mediation from an ultimate North Semitic source.[19]

The present writer believes that there is a preponder-
ance of evidence in favor of the early origin of Hebrew
eschatology. It seems likely to him that the eschatological antecedents must be found (just as some scholars
argue) in antiquity—in the ancient myths. But the
strongest evidence, he believes, is to be found in the
work of Amos—the first literary prophet. Upon the basis of Amos 5:18-20, which clearly reflects some of the
popular eschatological concepts, this writer would have
to date the origin somewhere in the second millennium
B.C. Indeed, it appears from the way in which Amos
deals with the erroneous popular ideas that the people
had *long* associated their own felicity with this coming
Day of Yahweh.

With the preceding definition of eschatology, together
with some consideration of its origin and history among
the Hebrew people, the writer must now turn to a discussion of the basic elements in this concept prior to
the time of Second Isaiah.

### III.  Facets of the Early Eschatology

According to Oesterley and Robinson, the following
themes constituted the earlier Hebraic eschatology: (1)
the Day of Yahweh, the time when God would intervene on behalf of His own people and would bring judgment upon Israel's enemies. (2) The hope of the estab-

lishment of the Messianic kingdom, and the rule of the Messianic king from the line of David. (3) And, finally, the restoration of the scattered people of God to their own land, and the conversion of the Gentiles.[20]

This first theme has already been touched upon, and will not be dealt with at length in the following discussion. The second theme is an important and interesting one and merits, therefore, a careful treatment. The third theme will, manifestly, not be considered here, but will constitute the subject for the latter sections of this work.

## 1. The Day of Yahweh

The Day of Yahweh was a central idea in prophetic utterance. But from what has already been indicated, there is still no solid agreement as to the origin of this belief.[21] At any rate, it appears certain to this present writer, upon the basis of Amos 5:18-20, to have been an ancient idea among the Israelites. From the popular standpoint, the Day was to bring severe judgment upon Israel's neighbors. God's personal intervention in history would assure this, and would guarantee as well that His people would escape from the conflagration (Zephaniah 1:8) that would consume others, and that they would share in the golden age which He would introduce.[22]

The prophets never rejected the idea of the Day of Yahweh; they accepted it. The important thing that they did do, however, was to moralize this belief. They taught that it would be a Day in which God's righteousness would be vindicated against sin, not only among foreign nations, but among His own people as well.

Thus, as long as Israel substituted ritual for morality, the Day of Yahweh would be the antithesis of the popular expectation—a Day of disaster instead of triumph.[23]

This moralized belief in the Day of Yahweh "formed the background of the prophetic conception of the future."[24]  Or, as H. W. Robinson says: "It will usher in the Messianic Age, as the startling prelude to the establishment of the Kingdom of Yahweh on earth."[25]

### 2.  The Messianic Kingdom

R. H. Charles agrees that the Hebraic eschatology centered in the "future national blessedness introduced by the day of Yahweh." According to the prophets, the coming kingdom would consist of a regenerated nation, a society that was moulded and infused by the very presence of God. This ideal society would be designated as the Messianic or theocratic kingdom.[26]

It should be said here that the term "Messianic" has a twofold meaning. The word may refer to the personal Messiah, or it may refer to the Messianic age—the coming kingdom of God.  In this later sense, then, the messianic hope, which played a prominent role in the religious thinking of the Hebrew people, is synonymous with the eschatology of the nation.  That is to say, it has to do with all that is directly related to the future history of the people of God.[27]

The origin of Messianism remains unsettled, just as does the question of Hebrew eschatology in general. Here, again, there are two schools of thought, the one holding to an early origin, the other to a late origin.

The Wellhausen school has usually regarded Messianism as a late development. As with the eschatological passages, so the Messianic passages in the pre-exilic prophets represent later interpolations.[28]

With this point of view Gressmann is again in the sharpest conflict. He holds that the Messianic antecedents must be discovered in antiquity.[29] The Messianic-king idea, he claims, came not from Babylon, but from Egypt, and was mediated to the Hebrews through the Canaanites.[30]

Knudson agrees that the Messianic hope has to be carried back "almost to the beginning of the nation's history." It was, indeed, an important part of Israel's culture—"the bearer of her higher hopes, the support and stimulus of her ethical idealism."

The psychological roots of the Messianic hope should also be noticed. These are the inherent discontent of the mind with the currently existing conditions, and the tendency of individuals to project idealistic pictures of whatever is distant from the standpoint of time. From the latter there sprang the widespread view of the golden age in the past and, by similar reasoning, the radiant picture of the glorious future.[31]

Although there might have been some borrowing in the development of the different facets of Israel's Messianic hope, there was certainly no borrowing of the hope itself! The invincible optimism that lay behind this hope must have been inherent. The same is true of those tremendous concepts which give perennial value to the Old Testament eschatology—"the idea of a divine world-plan, of a universal moral government, and of the coming of the kingdom of God."[32]

The prophets of Israel conceived of the Messianic

kingdom as an earthly entity.[33]   That is, they never looked for a kingdom beyond the frontiers of time and space, but they did expect a kingdom that would come to fruition within this spatio-temporal order. What they looked for has well been described as the "emergence of eternity in the sphere of time." Thus, they believed that Yahweh would intervene, and that His kingdom would be set up through His direct action, and would then be sustained by His presence.[34]

Finally, it must be said that in some descriptions of the future no mention is made of the Messiah. Charles is of the opinion that the Messiah was not an organic part of the conception.  In some places the Anointed One is conceived of as present and at the head of the kingdom.  In other places he is absent, and his place is taken by Yahweh himself, or by someone else.[35]

## NOTES AND REFERENCES

1. Nathaniel Schmidt, "The Origin of Jewish Eschatology," *JBL*, XLI (1922), p. 102; Hugo Gressmann, *Der Ursprung der Israelitish-Jüdischen Eschatologie* (Göttingen: Vandenhoeck und Ruprecht, 1905), p. 1.

2. Schmidt, *ibid.*

3. Gressmann, *loc. cit.*

4. Schmidt, *op. cit.*, p. 103.

5. T. C. Vriezen, "Prophecy and Eschatology," *Supplements to Vetus Testamentum*, I, Leiden, 1953, p. 223.

6. *Ibid.*, p. 224; cf. also G. Von Rad, *Old Testament Theology*, trans. D. M. G. Stalker (New York: Harper & Row Publishers, 1965), II, 99ff., for a brilliant discussion of both time and eschatology in Hebraic thought.

7. *Ibid.*

8. Amos N. Wilder, "The Nature of Jewish Eschatology," *JBL*, L (1931), p. 201; cf. also William A. Irwin, *The Old Testament: Keystone of Human Culture* (New York: Henry Schuman, 1952), p. 183, who says: "Eschatological imagery is just that: it is imagery. It is symbolic form employed to express the inexpressible. We do it wrong. . .when we take it literally as precise formulation of ancient expectations." For another good discussion of myth cf. H. and H. A. Frankfort, *The Intellectual Adventure of Ancient Man* (Chicago: The University of Chicago Press, 1946), pp. 3-18.

9. *Ibid.,* p. 202.

10. Carl Steuernagel, "Die Strukturlinien Der Entwicklung Der Jüdischen Eschatologie," *Festschfirt für Alfred Bartholet* (Tübingen: J. C. B. Mohr [Paul Siebeck] , 1950), pp. 479ff.

11. Gressmann, *op. cit., passim;* cf. also Schmidt, *op. cit.,* p. 105.

12. Gressmann, *op. cit.,* p. 236.

13. W. O. E. Oesterley and T. H. Robinson, *Hebrew Religion: Its Origin and Development* (New York: The Macmillan Co., 1930).

14. *Ibid.,* p. 342.

15. John Bright, *The Kingdom of God* (New York: Abingdon-Cokesbury Press, 1953), pp. 29, 30; cf. also Bright's "Faith and Destiny," *Interpretation,* V (January, 1951), pp. 9-11.

16. Julius Wellhausen, *Prolegomena to the History of Israel,* trans. J. S. Black and Allan Menzies (Edinburgh: Adam and Charles Black, 1895), pp. 414ff.; cf. also Kemper Fullerton, "Viewpoints in the Discussion of Isaiah's Hopes for the Future," *JBL,* XLI (1922), pp. 10ff.; G. W. Anderson, "Hebrew Religion," *The Old Testament and Modern Study,* ed. H. H. Rowley (Oxford: The Clarendon Press, 1951), pp. 283f.

17. Sigmund Mowinckel, *Psalmenstudien* II. *Das Thronbesteigungsfest Jahwäs und der Ursprung der Eschatologie,* 1922, cited by Anderson, *op. cit.,* p. 304, in a work unavailable to the present writer.

18. *Ibid.,* cf. also his later work, *He That Cometh,* trans. G. W. Anderson (New York: Abingdon Press, 1956), pp. 149ff.

19.   Julian Morgenstern, "The Historical Antecedents of Amos' Prophecy," *Hebrew Union College Annual,* XV (1940), pp. 284-285.

20.   Oesterley and Robinson, *op. cit.,* p. 343.

21.   A. C. Knudson, *The Prophetic Movement in Israel* (New York: The Methodist Book Concern, 1921), pp. 161-164, reasons convincingly that this idea may have arisen from a reaction of the Hebrews against the popular cyclic view of history, held by the ancient Persians and others.

22.   *Ibid.,* p. 163.   Cf. Morgenstern's eloquent description, *op. cit.,* pp. 286-287.

23.   George Adam Smith, *The Book of the Twelve Prophets* (London: Hodder and Stoughton, 1928), p. 173.

24.   Knudson, *Prophetic Movement in Israel, op. cit.,* p. 163.

25.   H. W. Robinson, *Religious Ideas of the Old Testament* (New York: Charles Scribner's Sons, 1927), p. 190.

26.   R. H. Charles, *Hebrew, Jewish and Christian Eschatology from Pre-Prophetic Times Till the Close of the New Testament Canon* (London: Adam and Charles Black, 1899), p. 82.

27.   Knudson, *The Religious Teaching of the Old Testament* (New York: The Abingdon Press, 1918), p. 351.

28.   *Ibid.,* p. 352.

29.   Hugo Gressmann, "The Sources of Israel's Messianic Hope," *The American Journal of Theology,* XVII (1913), pp. 173-194.

30.   *Ibid.,* p. 189.

31.   Knudson, *Religious Teaching, op. cit.,* p. 357.

32.   *Ibid.*

33.   R. H. Charles, *op. cit.,* p. 160, says: "The Messianic kingdom was always conceived as eternal on earth save in Isaiah LXV. 17, LXVI. 22, where a new heaven and a new earth are spoken of; but these verses are at issue with their contexts, and should no doubt be rejected."

34.   Knudson, *Religious Teaching, op. cit.,* p. 369.

35.   Charles, *op. cit.,* p. 83.

## Chapter 5

## SECOND ISAIAH'S ESCHATOLOGY

In the preceding chapter the writer has attempted to define prophetic eschatology, has traced its origin and set forth the principal elements in prophetic thought prior to the time of Second Isaiah. With this essential background, we can now proceed to identify the eschatological passages in Isaiah 40-55 and submit these materials to a critical examination. This exercise will provide the basis not only for a description of Second Isaiah's eschatology but for an interpretation of the entire prophecy.

### Isaiah 40:3-5

3. A voice cries:
   "In the wilderness prepare the way of the Lord,
     make straight in the desert a highway for our
       God.
4. Every valley shall be lifted up,
     And every mountain and hill be made low;
   the uneven ground shall become level,
     and the rough places a plain.
5. And the glory of the Lord shall be revealed,
     and all flesh shall see it together,
       for the mouth of the Lord has spoken."

History and eschatology obviously meet in these verses.[1] Although one cannot be dogmatic on this point, there appear to be two historical antecedents in the mind of the prophet: the exodus from Egypt, and his personal acquaintance with the processional street in Babylon, which had, incidentally, been dedicated to Marduk, along which the Babylonian deities were borne on festival occasions.[2] This processional way obviously reminded the prophet of a great highway, the kind that Yahweh could be expected to march upon across the wilderness as He led His people back to their homeland.

The following cuneiform inscriptions, in addition to being closely parallel with Isaiah 40:3-5, give a vivid glimpse of the procession of the god (or gods) on a festal occasion.

> . . .from hostile Elam he took
> the street of joy, a
> path of jubilation
> . . .of a favorable hearing to Suanna.
> The people of the land saw his lofty form,
> the ruler in his adornments.[3]

Verses 3 and 4 become much more intelligible when one remembers the ancient Oriental practices of preparing the roads over which a great conqueror or king was to pass. Yahweh here is the victorious conqueror who leads His people again (just as in the Exodus from Egypt) out of their captivity into a new and richer experience.

The reader should be reminded at this point that the Exodus is a primary element in the eschatology of Second Isaiah.[4]  It is a fitting symbol of deliverance and victory, but still a mere adumbration of that which will be experienced ultimately. Thus, in this climactic deliverance the angelic ministers might well be summoned to make the paths straight and to smooth over the uneven surfaces.[5] For in so doing they would be performing for Yahweh the same kind of service that human beings had long been accustomed to performing for the eastern monarchs.

Bishop Lowth declares that when Oriental monarchs set out upon an expedition, or even on a journey, especially through the desert or wild country, they sent emissaries before them to make arrangement for their passage. Moreover, he says, pioneers were dispatched "to open the passes, to level the ways, and to remove all impediments."[6] The prophet, then, could not expect any less for Yahweh in the forthcoming eschatological event.

Ulrich Simon suggests that the prophet's main concern in this proclamation is not with geography, nor the transportation of a group of persons over an imaginary highway in the desert which, of course, could have been avoided. This oracle, he says, predicts an "eschatological movement of peoples. . . . It initiates the great movement to end all movements."[7]

Verse 5 suggests an unparalleled revelation of Yahweh as a fitting concomitant of His victorious march at the head of the returning exiles. This decisive theophany would reveal that He was victor over His enemies. Muilenburg says:

> The glory that once appeared on the sacred mount. . . ,
> and later tabernacled in the sacred precincts of the holy

of holies, is now to appear in a final epiphany. . . . This . . .
theophany. . . is final and decisive, universal and all-
inclusive. It "fills" time and space. It is a world theophany
and comes at the turn of the ages as the fulfillment of the
divine purpose in history. . . .8

*Verses 9-11*

9.  Get you up to a high mountain,
         O Zion, herald of good tidings;
    lift up your voice with strength,
         O Jerusalem, herald of good tidings,
         lift it up, fear not;
    say to the cities of Judah,
         "Behold your God!"
10. Behold, the Lord God comes with might,
         and his arm rules for him;
    behold, his reward is with him,
         and his recompense before him.
11. He will feed his flock like a shepherd,
         he will gather the lambs in his arms,
    he will carry them in his bosom,
         and gently lead those that are with young.

The scene shifts in these passages from heaven to earth
—even to Jerusalem. Zion (Jerusalem) assumes the role
of a herald; she is to broadcast the inspiring news of
Yahweh's advent. To do this the most effectively, she is
directed to climb the highest mountain so that she can
be heard and *seen* by all peoples. Thus the stage is set,
and preparations made "for the vast panorama of history and eschatology which is to follow."9

Verse 10 is typically eschatological: Yahweh's advent

is with might and power—as victorious conqueror and Lord. He comes as king to establish His kingdom (52: 7-10; 41:21; 43:15; 44:6).

Verses 10b and 11 depict this triumphant One as the Good Shepherd, so far as His own people are concerned.[10]

Throughout these verses it is strongly evident that the eyes of men will not be focused upon the returning exiles, but their gaze will be fixed upon God![11]

Although verse 12 is not an eschatological passage, it follows logically (from the standpoint of Second Isaiah's eschatology) Yahweh's revelation and redemption of his people. For, as Muilenburg declares: "Beginning and end, creation and redemption, are the two poles of eschatological thought."[12]

## Chapter 41

Verse 4, although not necessarily an eschatological passage, presents a vivid insight into Second Isaiah's "theology of history."[13] The prophet asks a decisive query and then answers it with unquestioned certainty:

> Who has performed and done this,
>> calling the generations from the beginning?
> I, the Lord, the first
>> and the last; I am He.

The prophet is convinced that both past and future belong to God. The last things or eschatological events are not only embraced by His providence, but are comprehended within His purpose. History is thus of one cloth—there is no real separation between the beginning and the ending.    "Just as the creation is not to be thought of apart from its creator so the end cannot be severed from the author of the end."[14]

The background for the prophet's thought in chapter 41 is the sovereign, redemptive power of God as it expresses itself in history.   The very interesting point that the prophet makes in vv. 15, 16, before moving on to the eschatological section in vv. 17-20, is that Israel may be the instrument through which God will implement His ultimate purpose.[15]

*Verses 17-20*

17.   When the poor and needy seek water,
        and there is none,
        and their tongue is parched with thirst,
    I the Lord will answer them,
    I the God of Israel will not forsake them.
18.   I will open rivers on the bare heights,
        and fountains in the midst of the valleys;
    I will make the wilderness a pool of water,
        and the dry land springs of water.
19.   I will put in the wilderness the cedar,
        the acacia, the myrtle, and the olive;
    I will set in the desert the cypress,
        the plane and the pine together;
20.   that men may see and know,
        may consider and understand together,
    that the hand of the Lord has done this,
        the Holy One of Israel has created it.

Verse 17 compares Israel in her exile with "wretches dying of thirst. . . ."[16]  Thus God's promise is adapted to their needs, and His power assumes an apocalyptic dimension in that nature is to be markedly transformed. This, however, is a central feature of Second Isaiah's eschatology (43:18-21; 48:21; 49:9-11; 55:13). The pronounced emphasis upon the fertility of the land is also reminiscent of God's work in creation.[17]

Muilenburg admits that the "language of myth" is here employed, but that it does witness to subsequent events. He says: "To the ancient Hebrew, nature, like history, is the realm of eventfulness. It is the theater of God's activity."[18]   Cheyne feels that the language here is an expressive figure for the highest happiness.[19]   Skinner, too, suggests that the spiritual meaning must not be lost sight of in the midst of the marvelous description of the desert journey.[20]

Verse 20 reveals clearly the ultimate object of this great miracle. It is for the purpose of demonstrating to all men the creative power of the one true God.[21]

## Chapter 42

The first of the so-called Servant Poems is encountered in this chapter—vv. 1-4 (or possibly vv. 1-7). The writer has already given some consideration to the Servant passages in the first chapter of this study.  But since there are some critics who hold that the Servant poems are eschatological, it will be necessary to make some additional comments as the various poems are encountered. It will be evident, of course, to the reader that the present study will not allow a detailed consideration of this whole tremendous problem.

Paul Volz discovers two poems in the first nine verses of chapter 42: (1) vv. 1-4; (2) vv. 5-9.[22]

Although seeing a strong eschatological element in Second Isaiah, as well as in the other prophets, Volz fails to find an eschatological motif in the first three (he would say "four") Servant poems. Instead, he finds the poems to be autobiographical. Volz feels that Second Isaiah possibly abandoned the hope that he had at first in Cyrus—that is to say, in secular and political power—and came to feel that he himself was to initiate God's kingdom upon earth. Thus, the kingdom would not be initiated eschatologically, but would be realized through the Servant—even through the prophet himself.[23]

Rudolph Otto, on the other hand, espouses a view in direct antithesis to Volz's. Otto says pointedly that the Suffering Servant in Deutero-Isaiah "was conceived eschatologically throughout and was an *eschatological* redeemer. . . ."[24]

### Verses 10-17

10.  Sing to the Lord a new song,
       his praise from the end of the earth!
     Let the sea roar and all that fills it,
       the coastlands and their inhabitants.
11.  Let the desert and its cities lift up their voice,
       the villages that Kedar inhabits;
     let the inhabitants of Sela sing for joy,
       let them shout from the top of the mountains.
12.  Let them give glory to the Lord,
       and declare his praise in the coastlands.
13.  The Lord goes forth like a mighty man,
       like a man of war he stirs up his fury;

he cries out, he shouts aloud,
he shows himself mighty against his foes.

14. For a long time I have held my peace,
I have kept still and restrained myself;
now I will cry out like a woman in travail,
I will gasp and pant.

15. I will lay waste mountains and hills,
and dry up all their herbage;
I will turn the rivers into islands,
and dry up the pools.

16. And I will lead the blind
in a way that they know not,
in paths that they have not known
I will guide them.
I will turn the darkness before them into
light,
the rough places into level ground.
These are the things I will do,
and I will not forsake them.

17. They shall be turned back and utterly put to
shame,
who trust in graven images,
who say to molten images,
"You are our gods."

The new song of redemption in vv. 10ff. is a typical eschatological hymn.[25] The whole cosmic order is enjoined to raise its voice in jubilant song before the Conqueror's coming. Muilenburg is undoubtedly correct in assuming that the style and language of this hymn were influenced by the enthronement songs employed in the ritual of the New Year.[26]

Verse 13 gives the reason for the earth's being called upon to join in this "new song."[27]  It is to herald the coming of the dreadful warrior-God, who enters into armed conflict with His foes. There is never any question as to who the victor will be (vv. 13b ff.), for just as He triumphed over the primeval abyss and in the combat at the time of the Exodus (Ex. 15:3ff.), so He will achieve the same measure of success in the eschatological event.[28]

Verses 14-17 give a detailed description of all that the *Kriegsmann* plans to do. The realism is indeed intense. This passage evidently represents "ancient Oriental eschatological speech with all its rich mythological overtones. . . ."[29]  Finally, in verse 17 there is depicted the eschatological judgment upon the empty idol worship, as well as upon the pagan gods.

Paul Volz, with his unusually penetrating insights, summarizes Deutero-Isaiah's eschatological beliefs on the basis of vv. 10-17. He says unequivocally that Deutero-Isaiah is clearly eschatological. World events to the prophet are precursors of God's final advent. Cyrus, upon whom the eyes of the world are focused, is but a forerunner of the Day of Yahweh. For Second Isaiah God's coming is not in the distant future; it is this morning or this day! What he prophesied momentarily concerning Israel, Babylon, etc., constituted merely the first act in the eschatological drama. Thus, for the prophet, Israel's return becomes the world return. In other words, through Israel's fate the destiny of the nations is worked out. Israel's redemption and restoration to her own land constitute the prelude to world redemption and the establishment of the kingdom of God, or the world sovereignty of Yahweh.

It is indeed in the recognition of His lordship and world sovereignty that the whole world joins together in the eschatological hymn of praise.[30]

## Chapter 43

In this present chapter it is again apparent that the prophet sets his message of redemption within a "universal eschatological framework."[31]

### Verses 16-19

16. Thus says the Lord,
        who makes a way in the sea,
        a path in the mighty waters,
17. who brings forth chariot and horse,
        army and warrior;
    they lie down, they cannot rise,
        they are extinguished, quenched like a
        wick;
18. "Remember not the former things,
        nor consider the things of old.
19. Behold, I am doing a new thing;
        now it springs forth, do you not perceive
        it?
    I will make a way in the wilderness
        and rivers in the desert.

The overthrow of Babylon is to be followed by the deliverance of Israel. The method is again compared with the most outstanding miracle in Israel's past history—the exodus from Egypt.[32] The prophet's reasoning, it appears to the present writer, follows a logical pattern. The Exodus is the prototype of the last great (eschatological) deliverance.[33]

It is true that other prophets had recalled the miracle of the Exodus (Amos 2:7, 10; 3:1; Hosea 11:1; 13:4; Micah 6:4; Isaiah 11:16; Jeremiah 2:2ff.), but Second Isaiah is the first one to associate it with the eschatological event.[34]

The "new thing" that the prophet speaks of here has a rich significance. It is actually a summons to the people to turn from the past, freighted as it was with epochal events, to the more meaningful events of the future. Skinner says:

> The making of the way through the desert and water for the pilgrims to drink. . . is considered to be a miracle transcending the passage of the Red Sea, and all the miracles which attended the first exodus. This is the *new thing* on which the prophet's mind fastens as the symbol of Israel's deliverance.[35]

C. R. North is of the opinion that Second Isaiah believed the new Exodus would be "the eschatological culmination of the faith of his fathers." In one sense, then, the prophet was wrong, but in another he was remarkably correct. That is to say: "What he depicted in mythological language as the end, was, in its ultimate sequel and fulfillment, an even more wonderful beginning."[36]

### Chapter 44

The eschatological material in chapter 44 is very much limited. Perhaps only verses 3 and 4 will fit into such a context.

### Verses 3-4

3. For I will pour water on the thirsty land,
     and streams on the dry ground;
   I will pour my Spirit upon your descendants,
     and my blessing on your offspring.
4. They shall spring up like grass amid waters,
     like willows by flowing streams.

Kissane says that "there is an implied comparison in the two verses: just as water makes the grass sprout in the wilderness, so My spirit will make Israel multiply and flourish."[37]    Kissane fails to note, however, that these anticipated blessings, at least from an eschatological standpoint, are accompaniments of the new age.[38]

### Chapter 45: 1-7

1. Thus says the Lord to his anointed, to Cyrus,
     whose right hand I have grasped,
   to subdue nations before him
     and ungird the loins of kings,
   to open doors before him
     that gates may not be closed:
2. "I will go before you
     and level the mountains,
   I will break in pieces the doors of bronze
     and cut asunder the bars of iron,
3. I will give you the treasures of darkness
     and the hoards in secret places,
   that you may know that it is I, the Lord,
     the God of Israel, who call you by
     your name.

4. For the sake of my servant Jacob,
      and Israel my chosen,
   I call you by your name,
      I surname you, though you do not know
      me.
5. I am the Lord, and there is no other,
      besides me there is no God;
      I gird you, though you do now know me,
6. that men may know, from the rising of the sun
      and from the west, that there is none
         besides me;
   I am the Lord, and there is no other.
7. I form light and create darkness,
      I make weal and create woe,
      I am the Lord, who do all these things.

This passage which refers to Cyrus as the Lord's anointed has definite eschatological overtones. The primary question here, however, is Second Isaiah's actual estimate of Cyrus' role. Duhm contends that the enthusiastic prophet fastens his eschatological hope with reference to Cyrus upon an inadequately grounded intuition. For Duhm, Cyrus is only an instrument or tool for the execution of God's plans.[39]

It appears to the present writer that Cyrus' role was indeed instrumental. God was using him as His agent, but this is not to say that Second Isaiah misunderstood Cyrus' role. The prophet knew that it would be Yahweh himself who would actually initiate His great kingdom.

The misunderstanding of this passage stems possibly from the prophet's use of eschatological categories.[40] The present writer feels that this was only natural, for these were the normal forms not only for his thinking but also for his prophetic expression. God would indeed do great things through Cyrus, but all of these would merely constitute the first act in the subsequently unfolding eschatological drama. To describe those events associated with the Lord's anointed (vv. 2ff.), the prophet used categories usually reserved for the ultimate event—God's advent and the accompanying geographical changes.

Eschatological undercurrents are also detected in most of the remaining verses of this chapter. The three dominant motifs of such thought are clearly evident: creation, judgment, and redemption.

### Chapter 46

The eschatological passages are not too sharply defined in this chapter. However, Second Isaiah's "theology of history" is very pointedly and succinctly stated in verse 10. From this verse one discovers that the whole range of history is comprehended in the mind of God. History itself, moreover, becomes the arena for His action and concern, and ultimately for the realization of His purpose—redemption (v. 13).[41]

### Chapter 47

The thought in this section is quite clear. God is bringing chastisement upon Babylon, the oppressor of Israel. Cyrus' overthrow of this proud land is the prelude to Israel's deliverance.[42]

C. C. Torrey observes that Babylon was for the prophet "the typical embodiment of the worldly power and pride which he declares to be fleeting, and the moral corruption whose punishment he predicts."[43]  This same critic says that the word "fire" in verse 14 is "the standing feature of Second Isaiah's eschatology. . . ."[44]

## Chapter 48

This chapter is to be interpreted historically.  It has to do with the actual conditions confronting the exiles, and especially with God's providence, judgment, and unmerited grace which He directs to Israel because of His "name's sake," or "honor's sake."[45]

## Chapter 49

Critics are inclined to think that a period of time elapsed between the writing of chapters 40-48 and the writing of chapters 49-55.[46]  It has been conjectured that this latter section was composed under the influence and impact of the Cyrus edict, which permitted the exiles to return to their homeland.[47]

Skinner sees an advance in the prophet's concepts with the beginning of the current chapter.  No longer are the comparisons made between Yahweh and the idols.  Perhaps the prophet feels that his position has now been made secure.  No longer are allusions made to Cyrus and his conquest of Babylon, because that is now taken for granted.

Beginning with chapter 49 and continuing through chapter 55, the prophet concentrates his thoughts "almost exclusively on his central message of consolation, and the glorious future in store for Israel."[48]

The present section (chapter 49) does not appear to be eschatological.  The author does, however, reflect again his theology of history—the fact that God has a redemptive purpose in history, and is using the Servant as an instrument in the fulfillment of that purpose.

C. C. Torrey feels that this chapter occupies a central place in the book, since it projects the most characteristic ideas of the author with reference to the future. The first half of the poem (vv. 1-13) reveals God's purpose for the Gentiles; the remainder of the chapter (vv. 14-26) depicts His purpose for the Jews and for the city of Jerusalem.[49]

Verse 26a does present one common eschatological representation that is found elsewhere (Ezekiel 38:21; Haggai 2:22; Zechariah 14:13). According to this passage, Zion's enemies will be "consumed by internecine war."[50]

## Chapter 50

Chapter 50, although not eschatological in nature, gives reassurance to Israel that she will be redeemed. God assures His people that the marriage (covenant) begun at Sinai is still intact. There is no *bill of divorcement*; the children have not been sold to the creditors; God is not bankrupt. Israel has brought upon her own self the present untoward circumstances (Exile), but God can and will redeem the exiles.[51]

The third Servant poem is also discovered in this chapter (vv. 4-9). The suffering motif is prominent here, but the poem does not seem to have any eschatological coloring.

## Chapter 51

The eschatological imagery and motifs are unusually

prominent in this chapter, just as the following verses illustrate.

*Verses 3-11*

3. For the Lord will comfort Zion;
        he will comfort all her waste places,
    and will make her wilderness like Eden,
        her desert like the garden of the Lord;
    joy and gladness will be found in her,
        thanksgiving and the voice of song.

4. "Listen to me, my people,
        and give ear to me, my nation;
    for a law will go forth from me,
        and my justice for a light to the peoples.

5. My deliverance draws near speedily,
        my salvation has gone forth,
        and my arms will rule the peoples;
    the coastlands wait for me,
        and for my arm they hope.

6. Lift up your eyes to the heavens,
        and look at the earth beneath;
    for the heavens will vanish like smoke,
        the earth will wear out like a garment,
        and they who dwell in it will die like gnats;
    but my salvation will be for ever,
        and my deliverance will never be ended.

7. "Hearken to me, you who know righteousness,
        the people in whose heart is my law;
    fear not the reproach of men,
        and be not dismayed at their revilings.

8. For the moth will eat them up like a garment,
        and the worm will eat them like wool;

> but my deliverance will be for ever,
>     and my salvation to all generations."

9. Awake, awake, put on strength,
       O arm of the Lord;
   awake, as in days of old,
       the generations of long ago.
   Was it not thou that didst cut Rahab in pieces,
       that didst pierce the dragon?

10. Was it not thou that didst dry up the sea,
       the waters of the great deep;
    that didst make the depths of the sea a way
       for the redeemed to pass over?

11. And the ransomed of the Lord shall return,
       and come with singing to Zion;
    everlasting joy shall be upon their heads;
       they shall obtain joy and gladness,
       and sorrow and sighing shall flee away.

In introducing the eschatological promises in this chapter, the prophet engages first in historical reflection. His allusion to Abraham (vv. 1-2) is very appropriate, for the lesson to be learned from this story "is the certainty of the fulfillment of Jahweh's promise despite all obstacles." Although childless and old, Abraham nevertheless became the father of many nations. Thus, what God did for Abraham is an indication of what God can and will do for the exiles in Babylon.[52]

The promise to Zion (v. 3) is couched in traditionally eschatological terms. The waste and desolation in Jerusalem will be transformed into an earthly paradise like the primeval Eden. Paul Volz considers this to be a motif from very ancient times: the end-time turns back into the pristine age. The new paradise is the garden of the Lord.[53]

Verses 4ff. reveal an eschatological sequence that culminates not only in the assertion of the divine sovereignty (v. 5), but more especially in His "salvation-act."[54] Verse 6 contrasts the eternity of God—especially His redemptive purpose—with the transitoriness of material things, even though those things ostensibly be long-enduring, like the heavens and the earth. The same thought is evident in verses 7 and 8: the reproach and oppressions of men are short-lived in comparison with God's everlasting power to save.

When one moves to vv. 9ff., he discovers another place where history and mythology meet. The allusions here, drawn undoubtedly from the Babylonian myth, refer both to God's encounter with the inimical forces at the time of Creation and again at the time of the Exodus. C. R. North feels that the primary reference here is to the Exodus, although he admits that the original reference of four of the words—Rahab, The Dragon, The Sea, and The Great Deep—is to the creation.[55] The Hebrews, according to North's view, took fragments from the ancient creation-myth "like so many shattered remnants of stained glass" and employed them "to embellish the story of the Exodus."[56]

Volz, recognizing the influence of the Babylonian myth, says:

> *Rahab, Tannim, Meer, Tehom* are all expressions for the chaos out of which creation came forth, which the triumphant creator-God has overcome.[57]

John Skinner, in commenting on the imagery used

here in this mythological and eschatological passage, says:

> It rests on the conception of a conflict in days long past between Jehovah and the monsters called Rahab and the Dragon. Now both these names came to be used as symbols of Egypt...; and most commentators have thought that this is the case here, the historic reference being to the humiliation of Egypt, and the dividing of the Red Sea in the days of Moses.[58]

Skinner says further, in commenting on verse 10, that all the illustrations of God's power over the sea were, in a smaller way, a duplication of the creation miracle.[59] His power over the sea and His work in creation are exhibitions of what the "arm of the Lord" can do. This same "arm," according to the prophet, can be used just as marvelously in the miracle of redemption which is now anticipated.[60]

The principal eschatological section in this chapter has now been examined, but a few scattered passages still remain to be considered. The expression "cup of wrath" in verse 17 is a popular symbol employed by the prophets in their eschatological descriptions (cf. Jeremiah 25:15-31; Habakkuk 2:16; Ezekiel 23:31-34; Zechariah 12:2).[61]

Finally, in verses 21-23 a major feature of Second Isaiah's eschatology is portrayed: there is to be a reversal of present fortunes. The future offers much brighter prospects to Israel. Her enemies, who now oppress her, will be given the bowl of God's wrath from which she has been drinking.[62]

*Chapter 52:7-12*

7.  How beautiful upon the mountains
        are the feet of him who brings good tidings.
    who publishes peace, who brings good tidings
        of good,
            who publishes salvation,
            who says to Zion, "Your God reigns."
8.  Hark, your watchmen lift up their voice,
        together they sing for joy;
    for eye to eye they see
        the return of the Lord to Zion.
9.  Break forth together into singing,
        you waste places of Jerusalem;
    for the Lord has comforted his people,
        he has redeemed Jerusalem.
10. The Lord has bared his holy arm
        before the eyes of all the nations;
    and all the ends of the earth shall see
        the salvation of our God.
11. Depart, depart, go out thence,
        touch no unclean thing;
    go out from the midst of her, purify yourselves,
        you who bear the vessels of the Lord.
12. For you shall not go out in haste,
        and you shall not go in flight,
    for the Lord will go before you,
        and the God of Israel will be your rear
        guard.

In the verses above the prophet describes Yahweh's
return to Zion.   The ancient concept of the Day of

Yahweh, which received classic expression in the prophecies of Amos, Isaiah, and Zephaniah, obviously lies behind this imagery employed here. Second Isaiah conceives of this Day in terms of a universal or world-wide theophany. Moreover, "it comes at the end, fulfilling the whole of Israel's history and tradition (40:5). . . ."[63]

The vision of this eschatological event, which fills the prophet's soul with jubilation and excitement, is as powerfully portrayed here as in any other place in the prophecy. But still, in typical fashion, the Exodus tradition is the influencing factor in his closing lines (vv. 11-12).

Verse 7, however, reveals the possible influence of the Babylonian New Year's festival upon the prophet's thought. The Hebraic expression "Thy God reigns," or "Thy God hath become king," is parallel with the cultic cry of Marduk's worshipers —"Marduk has become king"—when this Babylonian deity was enthroned on New Year's day.[64]

Paul Volz says that the word *malakh* (king) is certainly eschatological. In the present rule of the earthly monarch, Yahweh stands silently in the background, but when the reign of God begins, Yahweh's lordship becomes manifest and He fills the world. Furthermore, says the same writer, this eschatological event is not merely an occurrence in Zion, but is of universal import.[65]

I. W. Slotki maintains that the perfect of certainty is employed in verse 9.[66] Thus, there are grounds for the eschatological singing which breaks forth, because God "has" or will comfort and redeem His people (cf. 40:1; 49:13; 51:3, 12; 43:1; 44:22-23).[67]

## Chapters 52:13-53:12

The writer has already indicated that it would be necessary to say a little about each of the Servant poems, because some scholars consider them to be eschatological.[68]     Therefore, instead of considering chapter 53 separately, the writer will include those verses in chapter 52 which are assigned to this last poem (52:13-53:12).

It should be stated at the outset that the present writer does not necessarily interpret the last Servant poem eschatologically.     However, he does agree with James Muilenburg who says that "the portrait of the servant's career from an eschatological perspective is certainly not alien to the context."[69]

Paul Volz, on the other hand, says pointedly that this section should be interpreted eschatologically.[70]

However, before Volz proceeds to give his interpretation of this passage, he summarizes its history of interpretation, and lists the scholars who have held the various views:

I.   Collective interpretations:
1.   Historical people of Israel: Stade, Wellhausen, Giesebrecht, Budde, Smend, Cornill, Marti, Konig, Holscher, Kohler, Fullerton, Skinner.
2.   The holy Israel (religious kernel): Collin, Knobel, Vatke, Kosters.
3.   The prophets viewed as a corporate body: Gesenius, de Wette, Umbreit, Schenkel.
II.   Individual interpretations:
1.   Historical person: Moses (Sellin); martyr

in time of Manasseh, perhaps Isaiah (Ewald);
Job (Cheyne); Deutero-Isaiah (Mowinckel,
Gunkel[2], Haller[2], Sellin[4]); teacher of the
Torah after the Exile (Duhm[2]).

2. Historical and also eschatological: Kittel,
   Rudolph.
3. Messiah: Rabbis of the 3rd century A.D.;
   Delitzsch, Bredenkamp, Gressmann, *et al.*
4. Ideal Hero: Gunkel[1], Orelli.[71]

In developing his own view, which is quite different
from most of the above, Volz explains how the great
prophet is moved by the need, illness, and sin which he
sees about him. He himself feels the longings for freedom and righteousness (justice), but he knows that these
things cannot be achieved through the instrumentality
of man. "All prophetic virtue cannot create or produce
the deliverance." The prophet believes that the human
need is too great, the sin too heavy, and the holiness of
God too severe for the transition from the present into
the new age to be effected through the work of man.
It must be through the work of God, in keeping with
His purpose.

Thus, according to this view, God takes the Servant
and makes Himself known. Moreover, He uses the Servant as an instrument through whom His deliverance is
consummated.[72]

Kissane, in commenting on the above view, says:
"Volz. . .makes the servant a purely eschatological figure
distinct from the Messiah."[73]

Slotki says rather pointedly: ". . .The servant is the
ideal Israel or the faithful remnant. That he is not an

individual is the opinion of all Jewish and most modern non-Jewish commentators."[74]

Kissane espouses the more conservative view and concludes that the Servant in this passage is the Messiah. He says, however, that only an outline of this figure is given, and one cannot look for the foreshadowing of all the details in his life.[75]

## Chapter 54

The historical and eschatological are blended in this chapter, so that it becomes extremely difficult to isolate the eschatological portions.

The following verses, however, probably fit into the eschatological framework.

### Verses 1, 3, 13-14

1.  "Sing, O barren one, who did not bear;
        break forth into singing and cry aloud,
        you who have not been in travail!
    For the children of the desolate one will
        be more
        than the children of her that is married,
        says the Lord.
3.  For you will spread abroad to the right and to
        the left,
        and your descendants will possess the
        nations
        and will people the desolate cities.
13. All your sons shall be taught by the Lord,
        and great shall be the prosperity of
        your sons.
14. In righteousness you shall be established;

> you shall be far from oppression, for
> you shall not fear;
> and from terror, for it shall not come
> near you.

Verse 1 may be construed as an eschatological promise, because Zion, now comparable to a woman separa-
ted from her husband, barren and without children, will
soon be blessed with unusual fecundity. This miraculous
increase in population constituted a major feature of
classical Hebrew eschatology.

This sharp increase in population will necessitate
God's people moving out into the larger areas (vv. 2-3).
Duhm feels that verse 3 is an allusion "to the restoration
of the Davidic monarchy."[76]

Since verses 11 and 12 probably refer to the historically restored city of Jerusalem (which the prophet of
course anticipates), the two following verses (13-14)
may do so likewise. But it appears just as reasonable to
think that they have a more extended (even eschatological) range. Thus, ultimately, the city of Zion will not
only be established in righteousness and freed from all
oppression, but Yahweh who is tabernacled therein will
be both Teacher and Redeemer. This will naturally bring
peace and prosperity.

## Chapter 55

Edward J. Kissane, in commenting upon the general
character of this present chapter, maintains that it forms
a natural sequel to chapter 54 which presents a portrait
of the new Zion. Verses 1 and 2 constitute an invitation
to the exiles to share in the blessings of the restored
Zion.[77]

These verses are not primarily eschatological; they are to be construed metaphorically or spiritually, just as Kissane declares:

> Israel in exile and longing for deliverance has been compared to people who are thirsty and hungry. . . Jahweh now offers not only to satisfy their aspirations (symbolized by the "water" and "bread"), but to give them blessings which are far beyond their hopes ("wine" and "milk").[78]

The present writer believes that the first few verses of this chapter are essentially historical, but without stretching the imagination too far he feels that they could possibly represent an eschatological allusion. T. K. Cheyne feels that the first five verses of this chapter form "an affectionate invitation to the Messianic blessings. . . ."[79]

Although some question arises about the first five verses' being eschatological, there is less to question about the last two verses of this chapter. The immediate reference of these verses is to the restoration, but the ultimate reference is to the eschatological event.

### Verses 12-13

12.  "For you shall go out in joy,
      and be led forth in peace;
   the mountains and the hills before you
      shall break forth into singing,
      and all the trees of the field shall
      clap their hands.
13.  Instead of the thorn shall come up the
      cypress;

> instead of the brier shall come up
>     the myrtle;
> and it shall be to the Lord for a
>     memorial,
> for an everlasting sign which shall
>     not be cut off."

Kissane sees a close relationship between verses 12, 13 and the preceding verse. He says:

> The purpose for which Jahweh has sent forth His word (11) is here described. It embraces both the deliverance from exile (12) and the future glory of Zion (13). . . .
>
> . . . The land now desolate will become fertile and cultivated. The *thorn* and the *briar* are the vegetation of a devastated land. . . ; the *cypress* and the *myrtle* that of a fertile land. . . . The changed condition of Zion will be a manifest and enduring proof of Jahweh's power.[80]

C. C. Torrey sees here a portrait of "the 'homecoming' of Jahwe's children of all the nations and races of the earth.[81]

T. K. Cheyne senses that the poetical figures employed in these verses are "presentiments of the Messianic reality."[82]

To the present writer, the transformation of nature is the best clue to the character of these verses. But at any rate, regardless of whether one agrees upon the nature of these verses, he must admit that Second Isaiah closes his prophecy on a tremendously high note[83]—with the liberation from exile, described in terms of the new exodus which is portrayed "in all the glowing imagery of nature."[84]

The poet of the Exile could thus say with a later poet:

> Earth and heaven seem one,
> Life a glad trembling on the outer edge
> of unknown rapture.[85]

## NOTES AND REFERENCES

1. James Muilenburg, "Isaiah 40-66," *The Interpreter's Bible* (New York: Abingdon Press, 1956), V, 427.

2. Reuben Levy, *Deutero-Isaiah: A Commentary* (London: Oxford University Press, 1925), pp. 114, 115. See the vivid description of this processional way in *ibid.*, p. 115.

3. Friedrich Stummer, "Einige Keilschriftliche Parrallelen Zu Jes. 40-66," *JBL*, XLV (1926), p. 172.

4. Muilenburg, *op. cit.*, p. 427.

5. C. R. North, *Isaiah 40-55: Introduction and Commentary* (London: SCM Press Ltd., 1952), p. 39.

6. Robert Lowth, *Isaiah: A New Translation With a Preliminary Dissertation and Notes* (London: W. Baynes and Son, 1825), p. 358. Cf. John Skinner, *Isaiah, Chapters XL-XLVI (The Cambridge Bible For Schools and Colleges)*, ed. A. F. Kirkpatrick (Cambridge: The University Press, 1898), p. 1.

7. Ulrich E. Simon, *A Theology of Salvation* (London: S.P. C.K., 1953), pp. 39-40.

8. Muilenburg, *op. cit.*, p. 428. Cf. D. Paul Volz, *Jesaia II (Kommentar zum Alten Testament)*, ed. Ernest Sellin (Leipzig: A. Deichert, 1932), IX, 4, who says that on the basis of Isaiah 6:3 this verse would not have to be interpreted eschatologically.

9. *Ibid.*, p. 431.

10. Skinner, *op. cit.*, p. 6.

11. North, *op. cit.*, pp. 40, 41. The same writer admits that this is an amazing anthropomorphism.

12. Muilenburg, *op. cit.*, p. 435.

13. J. P. Hyatt, *Prophetic Religion* (New York: Abingdon-Cokesbury Press, 1947), p. 85.

14. Simon, *op. cit.*, pp. 71-72.

15. *Ibid.*, p. 77. G. H. Box, *The Book of Isaiah* (New York: The Macmillan Company, 1909), pp. 189, 190, holds that Isaiah 41:11-16 is an eschatological section, but the present writer is in disagreement with him on this point.

16. Edward J. Kissane, *The Book of Isaiah* (Dublin: Browne and Nolan Ltd., 1943), II, 32.

17. Muilenburg, *op. cit.*, pp. 459, 460.

18. *Ibid.*

19. T. K. Cheyne, *The Prophecies of Isaiah* (New York: Thomas Whittaker Bible House, 1886), I, 258.

20. Skinner, *op. cit.*, p. 21.

21. *Ibid.*, p. 22.

22. Volz, *op. cit.*, p. 154.

23. *Ibid.*, pp. 149-167.

24. Rudolph Otto, *The Kingdom of God and the Son of Man*, trans. Floyd V. Filson and B. L. Woolf (Grand Rapids: Zondervan Publishing House, 1938), pp. 217-218.

25. Volz, *op. cit.*, p. 29; North, *op. cit.*, pp. 65-66.

26. Muilenburg, *op. cit.*, p. 471. This new song of redemption is reminiscent of Miriam's song (Exodus 15:21), which she sang in praise of Yahweh for His victorious deed in behalf of Israel at the first Exodus.

27. Cheyne, *op. cit.*, p. 269. Cf. Volz, *op. cit.*, p. 30.

28. Muilenburg, *op. cit.*, p. 472; North, *op. cit.*, p. 67.

29. Muilenburg, *loc. cit.*

30. Volz, *op. cit.*, pp. 31-32. Cf. Kissane, *op. cit.*, pp. 46-47, who is opposed to Volz's interpretation. Kissane feels that these verses are more applicable to the Exodus than to the deliverance from Babylon.

31. Muilenburg, *op. cit.*, p. 481.

32. Skinner, *op. cit.*, p. 40.

33. Volz, *op. cit.*, p. 36.

34. Muilenburg, *op. cit.*, p. 494.

35. Skinner, *op. cit.*, p. 41; Cheyne, *op. cit.*, p. 278, sees the glories emerging from this more decisive manifestation as spiritual. Cf. Kissane, *op. cit.*, p. 57, who shares Skinner's view.

36. North, *op. cit.*, p. 76.

37. Kissane, *op. cit.*, p. 75. Cf. C. C. Torrey, *The Second Isaiah* (Edinburgh: T. & T. Clark, 1928), p. 344, who thinks here of *"spiritual blessings* for the chosen people."

38. Cheyne, *op. cit.*, pp. 283-284.

39. Duhm, *op. cit.*, pp. 313-315; Skinner, *op. cit.*, p. 59; Levy, *op. cit.*, p. 185.

40. Muilenburg, *op. cit.*, pp. 521-522.

41. *Ibid.*, p. 542.

42. Kissane, *op. cit.*, p. 97.

43. Torrey, *op. cit.*, p. 368.

44. *Ibid.*, p. 372; Muilenburg, *op. cit.*, p. 551, suggests that this imagery is "drawn from the vocabulary of judgment."

45. Muilenburg, *op. cit.*, pp. 552-553.

46. J. P. Hyatt, "The Sources of the Suffering Servant Idea," *Journal of Near Eastern Studies,* III (1944), p. 79, note 5; Box, *op. cit.*, p. 239.

47. Box, *loc. cit.*

48. Skinner, *op. cit.*, p. 87.

49. Torrey, *op. cit.*, p. 380.

50. Skinner, *op. cit.*, p. 99.

51. Robert W. Rogers, "Isaiah," *The Abingdon Bible Commentary* (New York: Abingdon-Cokesbury Press, 1929), p. 660.

52. Kissane, *op. cit.*, p. 155; Muilenburg, *op. cit.*, p. 590, says that the miraculous increase in population was a major feature of classical Hebrew eschatology.

53. Volz, *op. cit.*, p. 112.

54. *Ibid.,* p. 114; Muilenburg, *op. cit.,* p. 593; Cheyne, *op. cit.,* p. 30.

55. North, *op. cit.,* p. 120.

56. *Ibid.,* p. 121. For a complete account of the Babylonian myth of creation see Alexander Heidel, *The Babylonian Genesis: The Story of the Creation* (Chicago: The University of Chicago Press, 1942).

57. Volz, *op. cit.,* p. 119.

58. Skinner, *op. cit.,* p. 109; Muilenburg, *op. cit.,* pp. 597-598.

59. Cf. W. F. Albright, *Archaeology and the Religion of Israel* (Baltimore: The Johns Hopkins Press, 1942), p. 90. The Ras Shamra tablets indicate that in the Cannanite form of this early myth Baal won a decisive battle over the sea (*Yam*).

60. Skinner, *op. cit.,* p. 110.

61. Muilenburg, *op. cit.,* p. 603.

62. *Ibid.,* p. 605; Volz, *op. cit.,* p. 121. See the interesting note in Kissane, *op. cit.,* p. 166, relative to the customs of the conquerors.

63. Muilenburg, *op. cit.,* p. 610.

64. *Ibid.,* pp. 610-611; Skinner, *op. cit.,* pp. 117-118; Henri Frankfort, *Kingship and the Gods* (Chicago: The University of Chicago Press, 1948), p. 326 and *passim.*

65. Volz, *op. cit.,* p. 121-122; Lowth, *op. cit.,* p. 392.

66. I. W. Slotki, *Isaiah: Hebrew Text and English Translation With an Introduction and Commentary* (Soncino Books of the Bible), ed. A. Cohn (London: The Soncino Press, 1949), p. 259.

67. Muilenburg, *op. cit.,* p. 612.

68. See especially H. H. Rowley, *The Servant of the Lord and Other Essays on the Old Testament* (London: Lutterworth Press, 1952), p. 85.

69. Muilenburg, *op. cit.,* pp. 632-633, feels that the eschatological framework deepens the Servant's function and extends his range of activity.

70. Volz, *op. cit.*, p. 189.

71. *Ibid.*, p. 188.

72. *Ibid.*, p. 189.

73. Kissane, *op. cit.*, p. 179.

74. Slotki, *op. cit.*, p. 260.

75. Kissane, *op. cit.*, p. 180; Skinner, *op. cit.*, p. 120.

76. Muilenburg, *op. cit.*, p. 634; Duhm, *op. cit.*, p. 379.

77. Kissane, *op. cit.*, p. 200.

78. *Ibid.*, p. 206.

79. Cheyne, *op. cit.*, p. 58.

80. Kissane, *op. cit.*, p. 208.

81. Torrey, *op. cit.*, p. 429.

82. Cheyne, *op. cit.*, p. 62.

83. Levy, *op. cit.*, p. 280.

84. Muilenburg, *op. cit.*, p. 650.

85. George Eliot, *The Spanish Gypsy*, Bk. I, cited by Henry Sloane Coffin, "Exposition of Isaiah 40-66," *The Interpreter's Bible*, V, 650.

## Chapter 6

## CONCLUSIONS

The careful and critical examination of the eschatological passages in Second Isaiah has given the present writer what he considers to be a substantial basis for the interpretation of Second Isaiah's overall thought. But before citing his own conclusions, it may be instructive to show the ways in which recent scholars have interpreted the prophet's thought. This exercise, we believe, will not only be revealing but will provide the necessary grounds (if such are needed) for this present study.

In the examination of this prophecy it has become quite clear that there are two principal schools of interpretation. One school interprets Second Isaiah's prophecies as highly imaginative (sometimes fanciful) poetry. Thus, the prophet's work is to be construed ethically or spiritually. The scholars in the other school, however, recognize in the prophecies the language of myth. They sense that the poet of the Exile is dealing with ultimate issues, and interpret his oracles eschatologically.[1] It is true, just as the following discussion will show, that scholars in the same school do not always agree precisely. Their problem is obviously that of semantics.

In our initial consideration, we turn to the school of

139

interpretation which has (until more recently) been the more popular of the two.

## I.   The Non-Eschatological Interpretations

As the reader will have noticed from the previous discussion, a number of writers detect primarily a historical or spiritual meaning in the prophet's lofty and eloquent expressions.  They readily detect that he had "a poet's wondrous language," and place emphasis upon the "music of his words" without, however, taking cognizance of the depth and range of his eschatological concepts.[2]

R. H. Pfeiffer, for instance, in discussing the style of Second Isaiah, makes much of the poet's imagination. He makes such sharp and pointed contentions that it will perhaps be better for him to speak personally:

> The poet's intense enthusiasm, fanciful Oriental imagination, and burning passion lift him above the world of reality to the realm of fantastic dreams.  He creates this Utopia by means of imaginative flashes and not, like some of the later apocalyptic writers, according to careful architectural plans and elevations. . . .  It is in vain that one looks for logical sequence and arrangement in his poems....
> His book is an incoherent succession of ecstatic shouts; his thoughts are poured out glowing and fluid, like molten metal before it has hardened into definite shape.[3]

Pfeiffer charges that the prophet employs the leverage of his imagination to lift himself out of the depressing present into the magnificent future which he sketches.[4] This same Old Testament scholar apparently fails to recognize the language of myth, which is an integral part of eschatology, and further accuses the prophet of extreme and fanciful exaggerations, the products of his "unchecked imagination (40:15, 22, 31; 41:4f.; 48:18f.; 51:23)." Professor Pfeiffer cites as examples of Second Isaiah's fancy the transformation of the desert into a garden comparable to the primeval Eden, and the picture of the New Jerusalem "with foundations of beryl and sapphires and with walls and battlements of other precious gems" (54:11f.).[5]

Although speaking in terms of the prophet's "unchecked imagination" and of his "hope in a fantastically glorious future," Pfeiffer nevertheless realizes that it was just such a hope that contributed to Israel's survival in times of unusual stress and tension.[6]

Johannes Lindblom presents some interesting arguments in developing the thesis that Second Isaiah was more of a poet than an eschatologist.

Lindblom feels that it is more accurate to speak of the prophet's view of the future than to speak of his eschatology. This critic agrees that Volz is correct in believing that "the idea of the ending of history and the appearance of a new state of things, described in mythological forms, is essential for eschatology in the strict sense." But Lindblom does not find this idea in the prophet. He agrees that the prophet looks for a significant change, but the new things do not mean the end of the historical process, but a continuation in an ideal form in Palestine, and in the historical Jerusalem.

Lindblom maintains that he can only agree with those writers who use the word "eschatology" to refer to the last things. In his thought, there must be a sharp distinction between the two ages in any eschatological formulation. In this respect, he is emphasizing a point made by H. H. Rowley,[7] namely, the *hiatus* which separates between the present historical order and the distant future or Golden Age.

Lindblom recognizes that the prophet speaks in terms of Yahweh's advent, but he doubts that this is an eschatological idea. For, says he, God comes to reveal His power; He goes out before the hosts of Israel; and in the cultic ritual (enthronement rites) He comes again to Zion, but these are not to be construed eschatologically.[8]

In his prophecy Deutero-Isaiah speaks of the judgment on the Gentiles, but this hope of Yahweh's victory is not of the universal, eschatological nature. It is merely the judgment upon the Babylonians, not upon all mankind.

This same critic argues that the references to cosmic events have been misinterpreted by the eschatological expositors.

> When we read in L. 3: 'I clothe the heavens with darkness, I make sackcloth their covering', the thought is not of future miraculous occurrences, but of ordinary natural phenomena such as clouds, mist, dust, sand, and similar causes of darkness. In LI. 6—'the heavens vanish like smoke, and the earth wears out like a garment' etc.—it is not said that the collapse of the created world is approaching, but that the salvation of Yahweh abides for ever, while the heavens are destined to vanish and the earth to wear out. The prophet is clearly familiar with a traditional, popular idea of the destruction of the world, and employs it in an antithetic comparison in order to emphasize the eternity of the saving work of Yahweh.[9]

The transformation of the wilderness is quite often

interpreted eschatologically, but Lindblom says this is just a metaphorical description of the blessings which God will bestow upon His oppressed people (40:3-5; 41:17-20; 44:3-4; 43:1-2; 42:15-16; 43:19-20; 55:12-13). Lindblom, like Pfeiffer, sees in these last two references especially "the highly-coloured language of poetry. . . ."[10] Thus, the conclusion is reached by this critic that Second Isaiah is more of a poet than an eschatologist.[11]

In addition to the other Old Testament scholars who have failed to detect the eschatological nature of Second Isaiah, there must be added the name of George Adam Smith. This expositor has written brilliantly on the prophecy, with deep insights and religious appreciation, but still the Old Testament student may well wish that he had detected the deeper or eschatological dimension which makes the words of the prophet even more significant.[12]

## II. The Eschatological Interpretations

Although he does not place as much emphasis upon the eschatological passages in Second Isaiah as do some expositors, C. C. Torrey would still have to be placed (it appears to this writer) in this interpretative milieu. In concluding his chapter on "A New View of the Prophecy," Torrey makes the following significant statements:

> In general and taken as a whole, these poems seem to have been rightly understood by the people for whom they were written, even if these were few, if any, who could rise to the full height of the prophet's conception in his

greatest passages culminating in chapter 53. His idea of the One God, his sympathetic outlook on the Gentiles, and especially his eschatology, depicting the end of the present age and the dawn of the new and centering in the person and work of the divinely anointed Righteous One, profoundly influenced the subsequent theology of his people. . . . In the New Testament the prophecies of the Second Isaiah are generally interpreted as they were intended by their author and in the spirit in which he conceived them, as truly "Messianic" from beginning to end.[13]

Torrey believes that the Messianic nature of the prophecy derives from the prophet's method, specifically from the arguments he bases upon history  In other words, the prophet's view extended from the beginning to the Messianic age, embracing as it did God's eternal plan for mankind. His prophecy is thus colored by the thought that he himself is standing upon the threshold of that day which he envisions as already dawning.[14]

Martin Buber sees something of the same thing that Torrey has detected in Second Isaiah. Buber feels that this prophet was the "originator of a theology of world-history." Accordingly, the prophet had no difficulty in believing that God could predict future events with certainty—for, in reality, it was none other than He who makes history, even as an active participant in it.[15]

According to Buber's insight, Second Isaiah conceived of God's creative activity continuing within the historical process. Thus, there could be no "theological boundary. . .between creation and history." Neither could there be a boundary between creation and redemption, for the creative process in history makes for redemption. Indeed, the transformation of nature is "symbolic of the spiritual transformation." But the most important thing of all in the prophet's thought was that ". . .Israel's redemption and the redemption of the nations are merely different stages in the one great act of redemption which God performs in the world of men."[16]

T. C. Vriezen also emphasizes the creative concept which he observes in the work of Second Isaiah. He cites the fact that the prophet uses the verb *bara'* more than any other author. This leads Vriezen to believe that Second Isaiah considered the salvation of Israel to be a new creation. Not only here, but in other areas the prophet could see new things come to pass which had never been before.[17]

These creative acts, according to Vriezen, occur within the historical framework of the world, but they definitely change the world. Vriezen conceives of this creative process as a kind of eschatology—an "actualizing eschatology." This kind of eschatology is sharply opposed to the transcendentalizing eschatology which conceived of an other-worldly salvation. In Second Isaiah, then, the Kingdom of God is not just something expected ultimately, not just something conceived of in visions, but it is something now "experienced as coming."

Vriezen holds that eschatology is more than a mere dream that is psychologically projected; it is actually a religious certainty grounded in one's faith in God. Thus, Israel's faith in its active Creator-God who works in history became the basis for its eschatological visions. These visions, in turn, became realities as the prophets experienced more and more "the discrepancy between what was and what should be. . . ."[18]

John Bright joins the above-mentioned writers in emphasizing the expected "new thing" which is so prominent in Second Isaiah (42:9; 43:19; 46:9; 48:3, 6-8). It is evident that the prophet believed the victory of God and the establishment of His kingdom to be at the door, for history is moving to its consummation; "the great eschatological drama is about to commence. It is as if the prophet were witnessing in the present suffering the birth pangs of a new creation."[19]

When one turns to the work of Ernest Sellin he finds a strong supporter for the eschatological nature of Second Isaiah's prophecies. In fact, Sellin seems to think that some interpreters have failed to do this prophet justice, because they have considered him an enthusiast and a visionary, not recognizing that the whole book is eschatological.

Sellin holds that, with the victory of Cyrus, Second Isaiah considered that the "Last Times which for centuries had been the object of a burning hope" had dawned. Thus, everything in the book is to be explained by this concept—"the miraculous march through the wilderness, the picture of the New Jerusalem, the conversion of the heathen, and the overthrow of the world-power (cf. also 49:26; 51:6ff.). . . ."[20]

James Muilenburg has more recently presented a viewpoint that is almost identical with Sellin's. This contemporary scholar maintains vigorously (and at length) that the form of the varied poems in Second Isaiah is determined by the theology which the prophet seeks to proclaim. In other words, the "general eschatological situation which lies within and behind the thought. . ."

has thoroughly conditioned the nature of this prophecy.[21]

In recognizing that the thought of Second Isaiah is eschatological, Muilenburg proceeds then to another very basic consideration, namely, the definition of the term. He says that when he speaks of eschatology, he refers to "the imminence of a great divine event which is to mark the decisive end of the age."[22] Furthermore, this same writer is explicit in detecting the major areas of Second Isaiah's eschatological thought: redemption, creation, and history.[23]

This coming of Yahweh may be considered a creative act in history, because it brings that which is "new," even the kingdom of God or redemption. Muilenburg detects, of course, that the imminence of God's coming is described in "Oriental categories of imagery." The chief one employed is that of myth, which (as has already been indicated) reflects upon first and last things. Thus, it is not surprising that one finds memory and expectation to be the two major psychological poles in the prophet's thought. Muilenburg says:

> His prophecy is an Oriental drama of beginning and end, of former things and latter things, of memories and expectations. Yet it would be an error to think of him as retreating from the hazards and perils of the present in order to fashion for himself an imaginative world of felicity. Nothing could be less true. Rather, he sees the despair and darkness of his times in an all-inclusive framework of divine revelation.[24]

The point that should be emphasized especially in Second Isaiah's thought is that redemption is eschatologically orientated. Muilenburg thinks that the whole eschatological event associated with God's coming is included in redemption. Thus he lists these elements:

1. Release from bondage—counterpart of Egyptian release (43:5-7; 45:13; 48:20; 49:9, 11, 14; 52:2-3; 55:12-13).
2. Judgment upon Israel's enemies (41:11ff.; 49:25-26; 51:23).
3. Return to homeland (40:9-10; 43:20; 49:11; 51:11; 55:12-13).
4. Rebuilding of Zion (44:26; 45:13; 49:16. 17; 51:3; 52:9).
5. Restoration of the land (44:26; 49:8, 19).
6. Conversion of the nations (45:20-23; 51:4-5).[25]

Finally, it should be remembered, especially with reference to Second Isaiah, that "eschatological thought includes within its range the whole of the past and present. . . . All the sacred past converges upon the present decisive moment in which the campaigns of Cyrus open a new era and prepare for the coming of the Lord."[26]

The present writer is of the opinion that an eschatological interpretation of Second Isaiah (such as that given above by Muilenburg) gives to his work a coherence that would not be discovered otherwise.

It should be strongly emphasized at this point that Paul Volz, the brilliant German expositor, has made a significant contribution to the eschatological understanding of Second Isaiah. Volz maintains that all the prophets of the Old Testament are eschatologists, but that this is supremely true of Second Isaiah.

In order to understand Volz's position clearly, it will be necessary to give a brief summary of this critic's controlling presuppositions. Upon the basis of Second Isaiah, Volz conceives of prophecy as the people's or the world's history, including the essential revelations of Yahweh. The prophets are His advance guards, heralds, forerunners, preparing the way, so that He can come. The coming of Yahweh "in a directly imminent historical act" is conceived by the prophets as the "last, conclusive advent of Yahweh."

Furthermore, the eschatological beliefs of the prophets apparently stem from their dualistic concept of the world. The world, according to this position, is in conflict with God, and nothing good can come from it. Thus, a God-pleasing human race could not be self-produced. Consequently, there developed the eschatological belief—"the belief in the wonder of the godly new creation."[27]

With Israel's redemption from Babylonian captivity, Second Isaiah sensed that the world history and the divine history had reached their goal. The restoration of Zion "goes over" to the establishment of the kingdom of God. At this point the prophet becomes "the definite eschatologist." This constitutes for him the beginning or first act of the end—not the form of the end in details.[28]

The main points to be emphasized according to the view above are as follows:

1. The final advent of Yahweh gives him victory over the world.
2. Establishment of the kingdom of God—some-

thing radically new has come into existence.

3. The final events are to happen in the immediate future.

4. The conquest of Babylon and restoration of the
exiles signal the beginning of the wonderful
transformation.[29]

C. R. North is another one of the modern scholars
who have been influenced by Volz's interpretation. He
says in a 1952 publication:

> The prophecy is predominantly "eschatological", i.e., it
> has to do with the "last things"; not "the last things" as
> they are expounded in Christian theology, but as the He-
> brew Prophet of the sixth century B.C. expected them to
> unfold. If we may use the N.T. phrase "the kingdom of
> God", . . . what is described is the coming of the kingdom
> of God. That kingdom is to come soon, . . .and its coming
> is to be complete and final. Yahweh is to lead his people
> home. . . . It is to be a second and more wonderful Exodus,
> accompanied by a complete transformation of nature.[30]

North believes that Second Isaiah definitely expected
something supernatural to happen. It is, of course, true
that the Hebrews did not make the sharp distinction
between the natural and supernatural that the modern
thinker is inclined to do. Everything had not been
brought under the control of "natural laws"; thus mir-
acles could happen, so far as Hebraic thinking was concerned.

The material element is noticeable, of course, in the
prophet's expectations, but it is not crudely material. In
the sixth century B.C. the belief in a personal eschatolo-

gy—life after death—had not definitely crystallized. Thus, God's dealings were principally with the nation and not the individual. The prophet, therefore, expected Yahweh to come in all the fullness of His grace and power. This, in turn, would effect the permanent physical and moral transformation of the earth.[31]

In a later publication (1955), North becomes pointedly emphatic about the eschatological nature of Second Isaiah's prophecies, and says that Isaiah's expectations must be interpreted eschatologically. Moreover, he declares: "I find myself entirely in agreement with Volz when he says, 'Deutero-Isaiah is shot through and through with eschatology. . . .'"[32]

North, with characteristic insight, sees the mythological nature of this eschatological prophecy. He explains that myth is "a description of something that lies beyond the horizons of any future we can envisage. . . ." Thus, he understands the new age which is so prominent in Second Isaiah as "the link between the mythological paradise in the primeval past and the equally mythological description of the paradise of the age to come."[33]

## III. The Present Interpretation

The writer's own study leads him to believe that the prophecy of Second Isaiah is more than utter nonsense, and that the great prophet of the Exile was more than a "morally deficient sky-gazer," as some interpreters have charged.[34] He does not believe, as some interpreters have alleged, that it was out of historical disappointments, particularly Cyrus' failure to become a worshiper of Yahweh subsequent to his capture of Babylon, that

the prophet turned to the eschatological hope in Yahweh's advent.[35]    Instead, the author of this study believes that the prophet, even from the outset, recognized
that he was dealing with ultimate issues, and thus his
prophecies were couched in eschatological language.

It is reasonable to conclude also that the prophet
recognized mythology to be a natural concomitant (or,
perhaps, a tool) of his eschatological thought.   The language of the prophet is not to be construed as "impas-
sioned poetry" only.   Even though one recognizes it as
poetry, it is more than poetry: *it is the language of
myth.*   Myth, then, as Frankfort defines it, "is a form of
poetry which transcends poetry in that it proclaims a
truth."   All the imagery that is employed in myth,
especially as it relates to eschatology, represents the
form in which that ultimate experience becomes conscious in the mind of the prophet.[36]

It is true, of course, that symbolism is employed in
eschatological thought, especially as the prophet describes in mythical terms that beatific estate which he is
conscious of, and which will be realized ultimately.   But
there is more to the prophet's language than mere symbolism: there is an element of reality—that which is ultimately real, even though it is not now experienced by
all men.

Indeed, the only way the prophet's experience of the
ultimately real could be conceptualized and communi-
cated to others was through mythical terms which spoke
of the sovereign and transforming power of God.   Thus,
Second Isaiah's description of the transformed, peace-
ful, prosperous land of Palestine is not mere fantasy, but

an actual description of material and spiritual conditions when God's sovereign purpose is achieved. The reason that he expects the conditions to obtain after the restoration can easily be attributed to his fore-shortened perspective.[37]

W. O. E. Oesterley explains well the reason that myth had such widespread currency in the ancient world, and thus why it was employed so frequently by the prophet of the Exile. He declares that myths were pictorial representations of ideas, and provided the means for the articulate expression of some of the elemental characteristics in primitive man. It seems that some of the ideas of ancient man, which were clothed in "the realistic garb of myths," were the normal channels for divine inspiration. The form of the myths seems to have been determined by the elemental human emotions, such as fear, the sense of dependency, and the longing for happiness. In the divine economy, myths were thus employed "to prepare and fit men's minds for the reception of abiding truths. . . ."[38]

It should be emphasized here that there were three principal myths in circulation in the ancient world, myths which are clearly reflected in the Old Testament: (1) Tehom-Myth; (2) Yahweh-Myth; (3) Paradise-Myth. These myths, it has been explained, corresponded to the three elemental human characteristics of fear, the sense of dependence, and the desire to be happy.[39]   All of these are reflected in the work of Second Isaiah, especially in Isaiah 51:9-11.

Just as the examination of the eschatological passages in Second Isaiah has shown, the prophet expected the imminent advent of Yahweh. This event would result in God's judgment upon all the forces inimical to Him and to His people Israel—reminiscent of the Tehom-Myth or God's decisive victory at creation. His coming would also bring salvation or redemption—reminiscent of the Yahweh-Myth, the belief in the divine being who is the embodiment of good, and who inflicts a decisive defeat on the primeval monster or forces which embody evil. And, finally, the return of Yahweh would initiate the Golden Age—reminiscent of the Paradise-Myth or the belief in the pristine age which would ultimately be restored. Indeed, just as T. H. Robinson has said: "Men readily transfer their speculations on the beginning of the world to its end; eschatology is the natural corollary of cosmogony."[40] This is precisely what has been observed in Second Isaiah.

It is evident to the careful student that the dominant motif in Second Isaiah is redemption. Although closely associated with the idea of creation, creation is subordinated to redemption because it is in the latter that the total purpose of God is realized. Indeed, "creation is [just] the initial act of which redemption is the finale."[41] Being thus primarily concerned with redemption, especially so because his own people were then in Exile, the prophet believed that God was about to act decisively, just as He had done at the Exodus. The first act in the fulfillment of His purpose for Israel and for the Gentiles was the restoration of Israel from Babylonian captivity. This part of His purpose would be achieved through the instrumentality of Cyrus, Yahweh's agent. But this historical restoration was only the prelude to the restoration or redemption *par excellence.* It is true, just as we have already explained, that the prophet was thinking consistently in eschatological categories, and thus to describe Cyrus' role and the actual return of Israel from Exile he used language ordinarily employed for the final, or eschatological events.

Then, too, just as has already been indicated, the prophetic concept of time was not so distinct as it usually is in the minds of modern writers. In the eschatological moment, the past becomes a part of the present, and both merge into the future.[42] Indeed, as C. R. North has observed: "The view of any great prophet is 'foreshortened'. He sees, inevitably, and with almost blinding intensity, the consummation as something near at hand. . . ."[43]

The teleological nature of history is evident throughout Second Isaiah. The prophet believed that ultimately God's purpose of redemption, both for man and for the world, would be realized. In fact, this ultimate purpose was inherent in His initial act of creation (46:10, 13). Consequently, when Yahweh made His final advent in might and power to establish His kingdom, not only would all inimical forces be subdued, but His coming would make for marked transformations in nature (40: 3-5; 41:17-20; 44:3-4; 51:3-11). Mountains would be leveled, valleys raised, deserts transformed into fertile plains, and springs and rivers would flow through arid places. When Yahweh comes all the redeemed ones will enjoy peace and prosperity (54:13, 14). *They will then know the full meaning of salvation!*

In summary, then, the present writer believes the work

of Second Isaiah to be eschatological. The immediate historical restoration, instituted by Cyrus at the behest of Yahweh, was an adumbration of the final events, a kind of realized eschatology,[44] which would be consummated by the actual coming of Yahweh in might and power to the city of Zion. His imminent coming would inaugurate the long anticipated kingdom of God, and would be marked by radical moral and physical transformations upon earth.

The minute details, which have been worked out in later Jewish and Christian eschatology, are not included in Second Isaiah's nationalistic portrait.

## NOTES AND REFERENCES

1. Kemper Fullerton, "Viewpoints in the Discussion of Isaiah's Hopes for the Future,"*JBL*, XLI (1922), pp. 1-19.

2. Cf. Julius Bewer, *The Literature of the Old Testament* (New York: Columbia University Press, 1938), p. 200.

3. R. H. Pfeiffer, *Introduction to the Old Testament* (New York: Harper & Brothers Publishers, 1948), p. 465.

4. *Ibid.*

5. Pfeiffer, *op. cit.*, p. 466.

6. *Ibid.*, p. 479.

7. H. H. Rowley, *The Growth of the Old Testament* (London: Hutchinson House, 1950), pp. 82, 83.

8. Joh. Lindblom, *The Servant Songs in Deutero-Isaiah* (Lund: C. W. K. Gleerup, 1951), pp. 96-98.

9. *Ibid.*, p. 99. The present writer fails to find cogency in Lindblom's argument, especially at this point.

10. *Ibid.*, pp. 100-101; Pfeiffer, *op. cit.*, p. 462ff.

11. *Ibid.*, p. 102.

12. G. A. Smith, *The Book of Isaiah* (New York: Doubleday, Doran & Company, Inc., 1927), II, XII-XIV. Cf. also Joh. Pedersen, *Israel: Its Life and Culture* (London: Oxford University Press, 1940), III-IV, 601-602.

13. C. C. Torrey, *The Second Isaiah* (Edinburgh: T. & T. Clark, 1928), pp. 75-76.

14. *Ibid.*, p. 68.

15. Martin Buber, *The Prophetic Faith,* trans. Carlyle Witton-Davies (New York: The Macmillan Company, 1949), p. 211.

16. *Ibid.*, pp. 214-217.

17. Th. C. Vriezen, "Prophecy and Eschatology," *Supplements to Vetus Testamentum,* I, Leiden (1953), pp. 217-218.

18. *Ibid.*, pp. 218-219.

19. John Bright, *The Kingdom of God* (New York: Abingdon-Cokesbury Press, 1953), p. 143.

20. E. Sellin, *Introduction to the Old Testament,* trans. W. Montgomery (New York: George H. Doran Company, 1923), p. 142.

21. James Muilenburg, "Isaiah 40-66," *The Interpreter's Bible,* V, 391.

22. *Ibid.*, p. 399.

23. *Ibid.*

24. *Ibid.*, pp. 399-400.

25. *Ibid.*, p. 401.

26. *Ibid.*, p. 412.

27. D. Paul Volz, *Jesaia II* (Kommentar zum Alten Testament), ed. Ernest Sellin (Leipzig: A. Deichert, 1932), IX, XIX-XX.

28. *Ibid.*

29. Lindblom, *op. cit.,* pp. 94-95.

30. C. R. North, *Isaiah 40-55: Introduction and Commentary* (London: SCM Press Ltd., 1952), p. 22.

31. *Ibid.*, p. 23.

32. C. R. North, "The Interpretation of Deutero-Isaiah," *Norsk Teologisk Tidsskrift,* 1-2, Hefte (1955), p. 139.

33. *Ibid.,* pp. 142-143.

34. Torrey, *op. cit.,* p. 18.

35. Sidney Smith, *Isaiah Chapters XL-LV: Literary Criticism and History* (London: Oxford University Press, 1944), pp. 18-19.

36. Henri Frankfort, *Kingship and the Gods* (Chicago: The University of Chicago Press, 1948), p. 8.

37. Cf. Millar Burrows, *An Outline of Biblical Theology* (Philadelphia: The Westminster Press, 1946), pp. 217, 218, who sees something of the same thing in Jesus' eschatological teaching—His expectation of the eschatological consummation in His own generation.

38. W. O. E. Oesterley, *The Evolution of the Messianic Idea* (London: Sir Isaac Pitman & Sons, Ltd., 1908), pp. 268-269.

39. *Ibid.;* cf. also T. H. Robinson, "Hebrew Myths," *Myth and Ritual,* ed. S. H. Hooke (London: Oxford University Press, 1933), pp. 172-196.

40. Robinson, *op. cit.,* p. 195.

41. Muilenburg, *op. cit.,* p. 402.

42. Cf. Muilenburg, *op. cit.,* p. 412.

43. North, *Isaiah 40-55,* p. 26.

44. Cf. C. H. Dodd, *The Parables of the Kingdom* (London: Nisbet & Co., Ltd., 1936), pp. 50ff., who popularized this expression. Dodd defines "realized eschatology" as "the impact upon this world of the 'powers of the world to come' in a series of events, unprecedented and unrepeatable, now in actual process."

# INDEX OF SUBJECTS AND AUTHORS